Jannes & Jambre:
Opposing Moses Before Pharoah

Learn how to recognize the last days' spirits that want to prevent us from being Rapture-Ready and choke the life out of us and our churches!

La Wanda Blackmon

Copyright © 2024 LaWanda Blackmon
All rights reserved.

No part of this book may be reproduced, stored in a retrieval system, or transmitted in any form or by any means—electronic, mechanical, photocopying, recording, or otherwise—without prior written permission of the publisher and copyright owner, except for the inclusion of brief quotations in a review. This includes information stored on public, school, and personal computers, as well as software storage and retrieval systems. All use requires written permission from the copyright owner or publisher, except by a reviewer who may quote brief passages in a review or use quotations in a book review. Contact the publisher for information about this title or to order other books or electronic media. Contact the publisher below for bulk book sales for sales promotions, fundraising, or education programs.

HFT PUBLISHING Inc

HFT Publishing, Inc.
P. O. Box 1863
Brewton, AL 36427-1863
Email: HFT-Publishing@post.com
Fax: 251-248-2709

Paperback ISBN: 978-1-953239-55-6
Kindle ISBN: 978-1-953239-52-5

Paperback Book Cover and eBook cover: Designed by LaWanda Blackmon with an AI-generated photo from Shutterstock

Interior Book design and eBook conversion by:
HFT Publishing, Inc.
Printed in the United States of America

DEDICATION

I dedicate this book to every Christian who has ever faced the opposing spirits of Satan—may the knowledge of this book help you destroy these strongholds in your life and help you to learn to live victoriously in these last days!

ACKNOWLEDGMENTS

I thank **Pastors Joey and Rita Rogers**, along with the leadership team at Pace Assembly of God in Pace, Florida. Thank you for obeying God and helping us remain aware of the principalities of darkness that try to stop every man and woman who desires to be used by God in these last days.

I want to extend a special thank you to Prophecy Conference 2024 Speaker **Shane Warren**, who listened to God and shared some valuable insights on the spirit of Jannes and Jambres during the conference. That was a witness of the spirit that this manuscript, which I have been working on this year, was "right on time" and needed. I had been doubting my timing for delivering this manuscript to the publisher. Thanks for obeying God!

La Wanda Blackmon

TABLE OF CONTENTS

	Dedication	iii
	Acknowledgment	v
	Table of Contents	vii
1	<u>Chapter One</u>—*Who were Jannes & Jambre?*	9
2	<u>Chapter Two</u>—*Why did Jannes and Jambre oppose Moses?*	41
3	<u>Chapter Three</u>—*What is the spirit of Jannes and Jambre?*	55
4	<u>Chapter Four</u>—*Can the spirit of Jannes & Jambre affect us now?*	69
5	<u>Chapter Five</u>—*How can we be protected from this spirit?*	79
6	<u>Chapter Six</u>—*Spiritual Warfare Prayer*	95
7	<u>Chapter Seven</u>—*Book Conclusion*	103
8	*About the Author and Contact Information*	115
9	*About the Author and Contact Information*	119
	References	125

CHAPTER ONE:

Who were Jannes & Jambre?

Jannes and Jambre may sound like unusual names to us. Most of us have been raised in church and have heard our pastors preach from Exodus and II Timothy, but we never paid attention to the names of these two magicians. We focus on the "Red Sea Miracle," an incredible story that builds faith. Today, I want to explore a different perspective on spiritual warfare from these two scriptures.

Although I had never heard a preacher discuss these two magicians, I encountered their names and descriptions of how they opposed Moses while attending Bible College and again in a spiritual warfare course during my ordination training. These two magicians opposed Moses during the "plagues" that God brought on the Egyptians. I never considered a sermon might less a book on this topic. However, one day, the Holy Spirit began dealing with me while I was in my "war room," completing my devotions and Bible study.

As usual, Satan tried to convince me that I was reading something into the scripture, but I made notes and started researching this topic in depth later that week. I was amazed at the information available online regarding these two magicians. The more I studied, the more I realized why God had laid this topic on my heart.

After about a week, I had completed most of the research. I started on an outline for this book and started writing it. At the time of the annual prophecy conference (2024) at our church (Pace Assembly of God, in Pace, Florida), I had already submitted my manuscript. However, if you attended the conference or listened to it via streaming (YouTube or Pace's website), you may recognize some of the concepts I discuss in this book. I felt that this conference was a witness of the spirit that my book was needed.

Each month, I meet with my editor to discuss the projects I'm working on and determine the priority topic. We occasionally adjust the publication timelines to reflect current trends or pressing issues facing the Christian church in the United States. If the spirit led, I have moved the publication date forward on books I was working on to complete another manuscript. I would have loved to add a few quotes from the Prophecy inference to this book, but there was no time for revisions and meeting the targeted deadlines.

I strongly recommend you go to the website for Pace Assembly (www.paceassembly.org) or to the website for Shane Warren's ministry and listen to Shane Warren's two services for the 2024 Prophecy Conference. You will gain a deeper understanding of how this spirit will impact the last days.

I have tried to keep this book short and straightforward. I do not want to overwhelm you with spiritual warfare concepts or spend hours focusing on demons. I want this book to encourage all who read it and help them understand what is happening in their churches. If we are aware of Satan's strategies, we can engage in spiritual warfare more effectively. We all want to live victoriously. We want to know that we are overcomers.

I hope this book ministers to you as much as completing the research has changed my mindset and the focus of my personal relationship with my Heavenly Father and His Son, my Savior and Lord, Jesus Christ.

Assessing Your Spiritual Life:

Before I delve into the identities of Jannes and Jambre, I would like to address a topic that can influence your understanding of this spirit. I want to discuss assessing your spiritual life with you. I encourage you to stimulate your mind to self-reflect on your choices, analyze your current situation, and be sensitive to the Spirit's witness regarding what is happening in your spiritual life, in your church, and within your family. If we are not aware of what is happening around us and cannot assess our current state, identify what is wrong, and determine what needs to change in our lives, then we cannot fully grasp the truth and concepts about spirits that are at work around us.

Our greatest tool in spiritual warfare is personal assessment of our lives, homes, marriages, and ministry. If we cannot assess, we cannot discern. Discernment is the number one tool for a Christian involved in spiritual warfare.

Relax. I am not about to launch into demonology or the spirit world of Satanic worship. I am not an "end-time" prophecy preacher or a "spiritual warfare" expert. However, I cannot discuss the topics I will cover in this book without addressing the end times, the rapture, spiritual warfare, and demonic influences. So, bear with me as I cover a few key concepts.

Assessing your spiritual life can be a challenging task. It requires you to be comfortable with who you have been, who you are, and what you desire to be—to have the integrity to assess right and wrong in your spiritual life. Most counselors and psychologists advise us to have someone we trust to be honest and open with us to complete the assessments needed. However, to be used by the Holy Spirit in ministry, you must first learn how to look at the good, bad, and ugly and make an open, honest, and objective assessment of where you stand spiritually. This needs to be done before you try to help others.

If you want to learn what God is trying to share with us through his word (the Bible), then we must be honest about where we stand. We cannot be defensive. I see so many people at the mention of a topic or demons go on the defensive, trying their best to convince everyone listening that they are not possessed or oppressed by spirits. They do not understand how the spirit world works, and they are insecure in their relationship with Jesus, so they become defensive. I want you to avoid this trap set by Satan and learn how to be comfortable assessing yourself or receiving an assessment from a seasoned pastor.

To help you learn how to assess yourself, I want to share with you what I teach my pastoral students in my ethics courses. I begin my explanation of self-assessment with a questionnaire that includes basic questions they need to learn to answer as part of their spiritual assessment.

Second, I remind them of the saying, "You cannot receive help until you first realize that you have a problem that needs to be dealt with!" A person with an addiction cannot get help until they realize that they need help. To reach this phase, most individuals must hit rock bottom. When there is no other option available to them except for rehab, they can seek help. This same phenomenon applies to assessing our spiritual lives.

Here are the questions I have my students answer in their "course journal." These are suitable for reflecting on our relationship with Jesus Christ.

1) Am I a Christian?
2) If someone else were assessing my Christian status, what would they say?
3) How would they substantiate the fact that I am a Christian?
4) How would they demonstrate or prove that I am a Christian?
5) Do I read my Bible and pray each day?
6) Do I look for excuses not to read or procrastinate by putting it off for a few hours?
7) When people come to me for help, do I know where in the scriptures to direct them to find the necessary answers?
8) Do I have the fruits of the spirit operating in my life?
9) Do I have all nine fruits of the Spirit present or just a couple?
10) Do I have days when a few fruits are absent during an average week? (example: patience and long-suffering).
11) Are there any works of the flesh present in my life?
12) Have I sought help to remove them from my life?

13) Am I actively working to change my character to be more Christ-like?
14) Do I follow the Ten Commandments?
15) Am I currently violating any of the Ten Commandments?
16) Do I fast at least
17) Do I love my neighbor as myself?
18) Do I pray for my enemies?
19) Do I hold grudges against those who have hurt me?
20) Do I seek justice or seek revenge against those who have hurt me?
21) Do I plan or strategize ways to make others pay for hurting me?
22) Do I talk about "my hurts" with everyone who will listen?
23) Do I spread gossip on those who hurt me?
24) Do I have a designated time of day to pray?
25) Do I have a designated place to pray?
26) Do I schedule time with God each day?
27) Do I protect that time with Him, or do I allow anything or anyone to interfere with this time?

28) Am I careless about what I allow my mind to feed on? (Examples: vulgar movies, secular music, etc.)
29) Do I feel that I am going to Heaven? Or do I question if I am really ready to die?
30) If I were in a courtroom standing trial for being a Christian, what evidence would the prosecution have against me that would prove that I am a Christian?
31) If I were standing before God's throne, waiting to enter Heaven, would I be allowed in?
32) If I think I would not be allowed into Heaven, explain why.
33) If God asked me to "List three reasons why I should be allowed to enter Heaven," how would I respond?
34) Does Satan fear me when I pray?
35) Does Satan feel that I am a threat to his kingdom?
36) Does Satan try to keep me from witnessing to people because when I witness to them, they get saved?
37) If God were to ask Satan if he had considered me like God asked Satan about Job in the Old Testament, what would Satan say?
38) If God asked Satan if I should be allowed into heaven, what would Satan say?

These questions are a great place to start with your self-assessment. Once you are more secure in your relationship with God and rooted in the Word, you can ask other close Christians to assess your life and provide constructive feedback. However, I do not recommend this approach for new converts or young ministers and pastors. You should be more concerned with God's assessment of you and your obedience to His commandments and plan for your life than with what others think of you. God's opinion of you is the only one that ultimately counts! Be careful of who you allow into your inner circle to advise you.

Reasons for assessing your life:

There are many reasons for us to assess our lives. The primary one is to ensure that we remain on track with God's plan for us. We must determine if we are following God's instructions and word, not man's interpretation of what God wants from us. To help us recognize areas where we have compromised. To help us realize when we have detoured from the plan or ministry that God designed for us. This will help us determine if we need to work on our "rough edges" or improve in areas where we struggle.

If we continually assess our lives and relationship with Christ against God's word, we will not wake up one day and wonder how we have drifted so far from God. We will see the slightest shift in our spiritual lives. We need to ensure that we are always shocked at sin! When we are no longer appalled at sin, we have begun to compromise and accept that there are situational ethics. There is no room for this in the devout Christian's life.

If Satan can desensitize us to sinful behavior, then it becomes easier for him to tempt us to sin or to compromise with others who are sinning. It becomes easier for a pastor to overlook sinful lifestyles and refrain from preaching on specific sins once they have become desensitized to the concept of sin.

The final reason for self-assessment is to prevent us from becoming self-centered, selfish, and self-serving. If Satan can get to be only concerned with what we need, want, or think we must have to fit in with everyone else, then we will fall into his trap of spiritual witchcraft. Not only will this trap lead us away from God's perfect will for our lives, but it will also destroy our peace and alter our spiritual path, causing us to no longer realize that we are serving God, but ourselves.

Why is self-assessment important?

We need to understand how to assess our spiritual lives and why we must frequently evaluate them to prevent being deceived in these last days. Knowing where we stand spiritually helps us keep our spiritual radar calibrated and effective. Without a strong and accurate spiritual radar, we will not recognize evil spirits that have infiltrated our homes, lives, and churches. Satan loves to get us to a place where our spiritual radar is off and the gift of discernment is no longer working in our lives. When we arrive in this place, Satan can take control of us. Satan also loves to get church leadership teams in this position. If he can control the pastoral staff, he can manipulate others within the church, control the finances, and prevent spirits from being recognized.

If a pastor does not recognize the spirits of Jannes and Jambre, Leviathan, and Jezebel in his church, he will never see the church split coming. He will be blindsided by the fact that he is asked to leave without any notice. He will not discern the child molester teaching the adult Sunday

School class, or the sexual deviant leading the youth, or the homosexual choir director. Satan wants to control these positions and influence the church of tomorrow. What better way than to "rock the senior members and leadership staff" to sleep spiritually, causing them to compromise and lose the power to cast Satan out.

A weak church leadership team means Satan has freedom and control in the church. Sin is not preached on, and deliverances are not occurring. Satan does not care how much you read and pray. He does not care about your good works and missions, as long as he can render your testimony ineffective and your spiritual radar incompetent.

Now that you know how to assess yourself and keep your spiritual life tuned up with God's word and your spiritual radar active, you can discern the spirits working around you. You will recognize Satan using the spirits of Jannes and Jambre to control new Christians and manipulate the church's leadership team, providing an open door for the spirits of Leviathan and Jezebel to come in and twist, confuse, and destroy the church from the inside. When this happens, the most organized, productive, and growing churches often split, and scandals ensue.

Knowing how to assess yourself before encountering the spirit of Jannes and Jambre is essential. These spirits will rapidly provide you with a spiritual assessment of your life, using it to manipulate you into their plan or scheme. This spirit preys on ignorance of God's word, operating with the hope that you do not have an effective one-on-one relationship with Jesus Christ.

The spirit of Jannes and Jambre manipulates the masses with "false miracles, prophecies, and words from God." It will use words of knowledge or wisdom that sound so similar to the actual word of God that most people will not recognize the difference. Like in the Garden of Eden, the serpent deceived Eve, not with lies or false accusations against God, but with "counterfeit words." Words that were so similar to what God had told Adam and Eve. Satan only omitted "not" while explaining the "why!" This reply seemed so logical to Eve. Even Adam was deceived by the subtlety of this play on words.

This is how this spirit operates. Therefore, you must be able to return home to your special place of prayer (your prayer room, prayer closet, or war room) and assess your spiritual life before God to recognize Satan's trick. The spirit of Jannes and Jambre is so clever; it can twist one or two words in a statement and completely deceive an entire congregation. They will be deceived if the church is not prepared and praying.

Now that you understand how to assess your spiritual life and why it is essential to evaluate and make changes regularly, let us review the two magicians mentioned by Moses in Exodus.

Who were Jannes and Jambre?

Jannes and Jambre were the two chief magicians in Pharaoh's Court during Rameses's reign. This was during the period when Moses went before Pharaoh, asking him to free the children of Israel from bondage (slavery). When you research these two magicians, you will find several terms used to describe them: False teachers, deceivers, influencers, opposers, and rejectors of the truth.

> **II Timothy 3:8**—*Now as Jannes and Jambre withstood Moses, so do these also resist the truth: men of corrupt minds, reprobate concerning the faith.* (KJV, 2024).

When Moses is writing the Old Testament books of Genesis and Exodus, he talks about these two magicians in **Exodus 7:11-12**. Moses does not list their names; however, Jewish history books and other documents from Egyptian history mention these two magicians that the Apostle Paul names in his letter to Timothy hundreds of years later. Due to time and page constraints, I will not delve into all the other literary documents that mention these individuals. If you desire more information or references on the non-Bible history of Jannes and Jambre, Google their names.

> **Exodus 7:11-12**: *"Then Pharaoh also summoned the wise men and the sorcerers: and they also, the Egyptian magicians also did the same things by Their secret arts: Each one threw down his staff, and it became a snake. But Aaron's staff swallowed up their staffs.* (KJV, 2024).

There were other magicians present. Pharaoh would have secured the most intelligent men of that day for his court. Due to the gods the Egyptians worshipped, I am confident that he would have also secured the most influential and educated holy men or priests for those gods to be advisors to him. During this period, it was customary for Kings to have sorcerers, prophets, priests, and magicians to advise them on all matters and decisions they would make.

Understanding this custom helps you know why Pharaoh immediately called for his "magicians" when Moses and Aaron appeared before him, saying, "Thus says the Lord God," and performing miracles. The Pharaoh had possibly seen those same demonstrations completed by his magicians in the past.

When God decides to send a message to someone, he usually presents that message to them in a language that they can understand. God even gives examples or demonstrations that make sense to that person. Geographical location and local customs can cause various actions to have different meanings for different cultures. I imagine that God chose something that would catch Pharaoh's attention. It was possibly a "miracle or magic trick" he had seen before.

However, God knew what Pharaoh's reaction would be—calling his magicians. This would allow God to take the next step and reveal to Pharaoh that He was the true God. I am sure you are familiar with this story and know that Moses's attempts to convince Pharaoh that the Lord God Jehovah, the God of the Heavens, was the one and only God were futile. Each time Pharaoh said 'go,' he changed his mind. Each time, the scriptures state that God hardened Pharaoh's heart and changed his mind.

Jannes and Jambre are mentioned in the group of "magicians" that Moses refers to in **Exodus 7:11**. Moses also uses the same Hebrew word in **Genesis 41:8** when describing the dream that the Pharaoh, who was in position when Joseph was in Egypt, called for the "magicians or sacred scribes" to interpret his dream. We do not know for sure which group Jannes and Jambre were from, but we know it would have been one of the following groups:

Wise men
Sacred Scribes
Priest
Holy Men
Wizards
Witches
Warlocks

> <u>Genesis 41:8</u>—*And it came to pass in the morning that his spirit was troubled; and he sent and called for all the magicians of Egypt, and all the wise men thereof: and Pharaoh told them his dream; but there was none that could interpret them unto Pharaoh.* (KJV, 2024).

<u>Recognizing people under the influence of the spirit of Jannes and Jambre:</u>

As I searched the scriptures for an example of someone acting under the influence of Jannes and Jambres' spirit, I found this scripture in one of the letters that the Apostle Paul wrote to Timothy. He was discussing this spirit with Timothy and explaining how to recognize it. This is the best way to describe how Jannes and Jambre acted or what their jobs included. As Pharaoh's magicians, they had pulled from their bag of black magic to accomplish what was required of them. They were motivated by the need for job security.

As you read the scripture below, you will notice that Paul described to Timothy what was happening in his church, outlining the characteristics that Timothy was to look for in church members who were under the influence of the oppressive spirit of Jannes and Jambre. You will also see some of these same characteristics in individuals influenced, oppressed, or possessed by the Leviathan and Jezebel spirits. It is incredible how precise Paul's description was and how "unchanged" it has become over the past 2000 years.

> <u>II Timothy 3:2-5</u>—*"For men shall be lovers of self, lovers of money, boastful, haughty, railers, disobedient to parents, unthankful, unholy,*

> *without natural affection, implacable, slanderers, without self-control, fierce, no lovers of good, traitors, headstrong, puffed up, lovers of pleasure rather than lovers of God; holding a form of godliness, but having denied the power thereof. From these also turn away."* (KJV, 2024).

After reading this verse, it becomes easy to recognize this spirit. How many of you have seen this spirit or persons under its influence in your churches? How many of you attend a church where this spirit is currently in control or represented in the leadership?

Whenever evil spirits take control or influence the leadership team of a church and its pastoral staff, you will find at the center one or more individuals demonstrating the behaviors that Paul described to Timothy.

When you recognize these spirits, begin fasting and praying for directions from God. You are about to enter a spiritual battle if you are going to save your church. If you are not part of the leadership team or pastoral staff, you must begin praying for them. If God reveals to you that you are in a church where the leaders are unwilling to change or cast out these spirits, then you need to pray for guidance on when to leave and where to go. You do not need to stay in a church under the control of these spirits, even if you are a seasoned Christian with 40 years of experience fighting the devil. Learn to be defensive. Protect your heart, mind, and family!

Many churches have leadership teams driven by pride, haughtiness, a love for money, and a self-centered attitude, which prevents them from showing compassion to their church members, let alone their community and neighbors. Even church members not part of the leadership team or board can become so caught up in their control or involvement in church operations that the spirit of power and haughtiness can be seen at work through them, influencing the pastor and board.

The Bible speaks of false prophets and teachers. The Old Testament books of prophecy and the New Testament book of Revelation warn of false prophets who will arise in the last days. These false teachers will possess such charisma that they can deceive devout Christians and sway the minds of new, young converts who are not grounded in the Word (the Bible).

Deception is Satan's number one tool in his toolbox. He uses deception in every task and trains each category of demons to utilize deception to their advantage. The Bible teaches us that Satan is the father of lies and that the truth is not in him. Knowing this about Satan and how his demons are trained will help you to recognize the works of Satan. Many Christians come in the name of sympathy, desiring to pray and support people to earn their confidence. Once their trust has been gained, these false teachers can often turn usually solid Christians into fearful, doubtful individuals who run in fear.

In most cases, it is easier to believe a lie than the truth. It is incredible how easily one can convince oneself that something is true or that gossip is accurate—Satan is aware of this fact as well. That is why Satan often uses deception through individuals who have worked in their churches and groups. Satan is the master of manipulation, loving to deceive and manipulate people to turn them away from the truth.

What is the spirit of Jannes and Jambre?

The spirit of Jannes and Jambre is a spirit of opposition with a tri-fold purpose. Below is a brief summary of the tri-fold outreaches of this spirit.

1) The first part of this "tri-fold spirit" is the spirit of opposition. The spirit of Jannes and Jambres will oppose you, as it opposed Moses and Aaron in Pharaoh's court. It **oppresses by discrediting** ministries, ministers, and prophets as a destructive spirit, rendering them ineffective. The goal of this spirit is to discredit you to the point that you look confused and crazy. If it cannot succeed with turning everyone away from listening to you because you are crazy, then it will begin accusing you of being a false teacher, a false prophet, or a lying pastor! If this spirit cannot stop you, then the next best thing is to ensure that no one will listen to you or accept anything you say. This spirit's primary focus is on opposing the person it is attacking to the point that they will give up and go away.

2) This spirit is a *"triple-agent"* spirit. It plays both sides of the church confusion, deceiving the pastor, board members, and anyone who will listen. Then it generates the third side or cover that makes it appear to be the perfect mediator or resolution expert for the chaos, confusion, and church-splits it has caused.

3) This spirit loves to act extremely spiritual. It will convince you that it has so much power and that the Holy Ghost moves on them, witnesses to them, and even gives them the power of discernment. It is part of its third cover. But this form of godliness is only to cover up the fact that it is a saboteur.

At times, this spirit has a fourth side where it uses your closest friends and family to destroy you. The strategy it uses most often is making constant accusations that the person is lying, stretching the truth, or exaggerating. If that doesn't discredit you and make people walk away or ignore you, he uses a family member to say things in front of the people he has recently tried to discredit.

Those family members are innocent of what they have said. They are not often cutting you down, but it sounds that way because of what those individuals have just heard about you. Under any other circumstances, the individuals Satan is trying to discredit you to would not have taken your family members' comments as unfavorable. Under any other circumstances, it would have been taken as a compliment or a joke.

Terminology Clarifications:

Most southerners call the characteristics of this spirit of Jannes and Jambre a "two-faced" spirit. Where I went to college and received my minister/missionary training, I was taught that a "two-faced" spirit is the closed-closet homosexual spirit. This two-faced terminology comes from the native American Indian culture for the spirit that allowed some of their "holy men" to be both male and female. So, regardless of where you live or the culture in which you grew up, know that this spirit is difficult to put into words. So, I prefer to call it a **_"triple-agent" spirit_**, because this spirit works through three main avenues in an attempt to convince all parties that it is on their side. This spirit is a master at getting people to believe in it and to trust it. It will create confusion within the church, and then step in, convincing the board and the pastor that it is the perfect resolution specialist or mediator. When the only thing it is trying to do is discredit the pastor and church board, destroy the church, and gain control of the pulpit.

I have seen this spirit at work through the associate pastors' wives in churches where the associate pastor was not chosen to be the lead pastor or executive pastor. When another pastor is brought in, this spirit begins its work. It will be the "best friend" of the new pastor, while fueling the flames with all who have ever been disgruntled in the church in the past.

Word of Warning About Words from God:

This past year, I witnessed this spirit at work in a church of approximately 2,500 members. I witnessed the wife of the second-most-senior associate pastor, who had sat dormant for six years in that church, weaving her web. She had convinced the majority of the church that she was the hardest worker, the most loyal, and that her husband was the only one qualified to run the church. In her final negotiations before publicly demonstrating her opposition to the lead pastor, she formed a fourth group—two-faced—pulling together a group of people who were unhappy with the construction changes, choir, praise and worship team changes, and how the pastor's wife was operating the ladies' ministry.

The pastor's wife thought this lady was her best friend. She had allowed this spirit to enter her inner circle. She also had the youth pastor's wife in her circle, gathering all the information from them, while she was convincing the fourth group of disgruntled people that if they would help her influence the board to remove the senior pastor and the youth pastor. She had them convinced that they needed to appoint her husband as lead pastor. She assured them that if they would appoint her husband, she would make sure that all the changes they wanted were implemented. She promised these ladies and their husbands board positions, leadership roles, and so on. She even bribed a few widows with money, flattery, flowers, and gifts.

I warned the pastor of this church about what God had shown me. He could not believe it. This spirit had him so deceived that he and his wife went for over a year without any contact with my husband and me. They thought I was wrong. They thought I was seeing "spirits and demons" where they did not exist. I must admit it did look as though this hard-working pastor's wife, who was not on the church's payroll (just her husband was on the payroll), could not be causing confusion or being used by evil spirits to destroy the church.

However, one day they woke up. I watched as the pastor's wife had a heart attack and died. Through all this drama, the pastor was put out, the youth pastor was accused of a crime he had not committed, and was arrested. His wife left him. The church split into four groups, with over half of the congregation leaving, and the two remaining groups were constantly at odds. They could not agree on a pastor. It was a mess, and the church split in two.

My husband and I prayed and prayed with this Pastor as he was broken and distraught. As I was praying, begging God to work a miracle for him, I even told God that I would start a fast the next day. To give me strength and during the fast to show me how to advise this pastor. Then the Holy Ghost spoke to me and said, "Get up. Stop praying. Do not start a fast. It is too late. I have already spoken. I sent you to this church with the message. But the Pastor rejected it. The spirit now controls the church. It cannot be reversed because the only people let in the church are now under the control of this spirit. Shake the dust from your hands and feet and walk away. I have written 'Ichabod' over the door. Tell Pastor X to get up, dry his tears, and move on. He will have to start over somewhere else. There is no hope for this church now. It is too late!"

When I gave this message to the pastor, even my own mother thought I was wrong. She told me, "That cannot be true. In the last few weeks, several people have been saved and filled with the Holy Ghost in that church. It is growing. Are you sure that God spoke to you?" I informed Momma to wait. I told her to give it 40 weeks, and you will see what is happening. Somewhere between three and four years from that day, the doors of this church will close. Exactly 40 months from the time that I spoke those words to her, the doors of that church closed. During its last year of operation, fewer than 25 people attended, and they were unable to find a pastor.

If you do not remember anything from the stories I share in this book, remember one thing: ***never reject a word from God***. Even if you do not like the messenger, or you feel that the messenger is a false prophet. Accept the message or warning with respect. Please write it down on a piece of paper or type it into your computer. Save the document and file it. Please indicate the date the message was given and who gave it to you.

In 40 days, go back and read the word from God. If unfulfilled, wait till it has been 40 weeks, and re-read it. If still unfulfilled, then wait until it has been 40 months. When you read it on the 40th month, if it has not happened, lay it aside and leave it there. Forty years is a generation to God. Sometimes, God gives a 40-year probationary period in the church, as He did with the children of Israel who exited Egypt. God allows a generation to die out and then raises a new generation that believes in Him with faith to carry out His work.

<u>Never put your hand on God's anointed</u>—even the ones you think are not anointed. We do not see what God sees—to discredit a man or woman of God can be damnation to you spiritually and physically. Let God be the judge. If you see the prophetic word or warning come to pass, then share with the world what has happened.

People are so afraid to share what God has done. Many people think that others will judge them as being "so spiritually minded that they are no earthly good" (my grandmother's favorite assessment phrase. Do not be ashamed of Jesus Christ, the Holy Spirit, and the works of the Heavenly Father. The stories you share may prevent someone else from falling into a snare. We learn more from stories and examples of how God moves, witnesses, and deals with us than we do from most sermons. Stories are more relatable. Remember, we must be vigilant against this "triple-agent" spirit, but do not let your discernment lead you to become a sinister church member or pastor.

Characteristics and Actions of this "Triple-Agent" Spirit:

The "triple-agent" opposing spirit of Jannes and Jambre has some unique characteristics that we can always look for—you do not have to be a pastor or have the gift of discernment to recognize this spirit. However, you need to always be on guard when you are at church or around other people, as you may encounter the following actions, attitudes, behaviors, and so on.

1) Loud, boisterous attitude—especially with women
2) Loud, flirty, clowning, center of attention, making the gathering about them, spirit—can be seen in men and women.
3) People who talk out in the service while the preacher is preaching. Disrupting the people around them. It does this to distract and keep others from getting key words or messages from God.
4) Controlling attitudes—individuals who feel that the church meeting or Sunday School class should follow the outline and discuss the things they think are essential, regardless of the agenda or the Sunday school literature outline.
5) People who get angry easily, pop off judgmentally, and show out.
6) Individuals who are haughty, unthankful, grumblers, gossipers, and slanderers.
7) They would rather tell bad news. They glory in boasting about something bad that is happening to someone else. Then they will say, "Oh, now I want you to know I was not gossiping. I am simply asking you guys to pray for them. I am so concerned about them!"
8) They love themselves. They love money. They are always talking about what they need and how they deserve it. If they cannot get what they want, their favorite sentences start with, "It is so unfair!

9) Every time you see them, they are boasting about what they have, what they are getting, and what they want.
10) Watch their relationship with their parents and their children. Most of the time, you will see that the children of these individuals are not Christians and will not have anything to do with the church or God.
11) These are the masculine women and the feminine men. The "homosexual" spirit loves to accompany the spirits of Jannes and Jambre and the spirit of Jezebel. This homosexual demon prefers to destroy a home and church over all other activities, especially churches where the pastor preaches against alternative lifestyles.
12) These are the individuals who will tell you it is okay for a wife to be like the gay lover her husband desires. The Apostle Paul called this the unholy, without natural affection, use of a man or woman with a lust not intended by God. (I realize that some readers of this book will disagree with me on this topic. If you would like the scriptures and research I have on this topic, please send me an email. I will be happy to share. Due to page constraints, I cannot go into details about this in this book.)

However, if your pastor tells you that it is okay for you to have oral sex, find a new church and a new pastor—they are already deceived and possessed by the homosexual demon. This is not God's intended use for the woman or man. This is not the type of marriage God intended when he created Adam and Eve.
13) These individuals lack self-control or restraint. If they want something they have to have it now. I am looking forward to it going on sale. They are considered impulse buyers. They will pay double the price for something to be the first one in their community or church to own the new technology, vehicle, or tool.
14) These individuals love to slander others and deny the power of God that is at work in those individuals' lives. They also hold grudges and love to seek revenge. They are sneaky with their revengeful actions. You will never see them coming for you.
15) They are headstrong, proud, and traitors. They do not love good, even though it appears that they do and that they are about good works.
16) Their actions are sometimes swift and fierce when they attack. They quickly repent, saying their temper got the best of them, only as a cover. It is not from their hearts. This is evident because they continue without self-control, repeating the same actions or experiencing the same types of outbursts frequently.
17) Their outbursts are with fierce anger, loud, and boisterous.

18) They are about pleasure. They cannot have enough "toys." Their plans are always about what they want or need, never about missions or what is best for the church or community.
19) They will appear to be the godliest women in the church. If it is a man, he will appear to be the strictest, most holy man, if that is what is needed to deceive the people around them and ensure that their "triple-agent" cover is intact.
20) Otherwise, these individuals will be among the most liberal members of the church. Wanting everyone to be woke and tolerant. They cry "legalism" and accuse everyone around them of being legalistic if it appears that the Sunday school teacher or preacher is going to preach on consecration.
21) If you watch their personal life, you will notice that they do not have a designated time to read and pray. They will be so busy doing "works" at the church that these individuals will sometimes go the whole week without opening their Bibles between services.
22) The Apostle Paul said to watch for the individuals holding a "form of godliness, but who have denied the power thereof—to turn away from them!"
23) Watch the people who try to convince you that all this emotionalism, shouting, talking in tongues, prophecy, and lengthy altar services are not necessary.
24) These individuals quickly speak doom over anyone they feel threatened by or anyone they think might get closer to the pastor than they are…just another form of "control."
25) If you watch closely, you will see the characteristics of the spirits of Leviathan, Python, and Jezebel active in their lives before they launch their "full-blown" attack on the pastor and devout Christians.

Remember that the spirit of Jannes and Jambres began with opposing men and women of God, just as it did when it opposed Moses and Aaron before Pharaoh. If this spirit can get you to give up and walk away, he is satisfied with his results and will usually move on to attack someone else. However, as honest men and women of God called to ministry, we initially "fight back" to defend our field or "pea patch" (More on this later—see chapter six).

Resisting Satan and this spirit:

If we resist the devil, he gathers the "department heads" in hell. He strategizes how best to hinder our work for God or to undermine our effectiveness by destroying our reputations. The harder we resist the devil, the stronger the warfare becomes. This is why many people give up early in the battle. They do not want to suffer, be defamed, or fight daily to achieve victory.

I can hear some of you say, "Why on earth would I continue to fight with or resist the devil daily? Why not let them have whoever and whatever they want? Why not let someone else have this ministry? All I want is to be a good Christian, live a moral life, and be rapture-ready or ready to go by the way of the grave if necessary!" This is a typical response for our human minds. However, we must remember that Jesus never promised us an easy life.

The scripture tells us that the world hated Jesus and that it will hate us even more. Jesus also said he was returning to the Father, so we could do even more than he did when he was here on earth. If we are going to be anointed to do even more, then it is only to be expected that Satan will fight us harder and with more vigor than he did Jesus during the thirty-three years he was on earth.

Satan had many men who falsely accused Jesus of various crimes and false prophecies. Satan mobilized the religious leaders against Jesus by using fear to try to stomp out Jesus' influence. The opposing spirit of Jannes and Jambres was very much alive during Jesus' time on earth. Satan tried extensively to destroy Jesus' reputation! This spirit convinced Caiaphas and the Sanhedrin court that Jesus was going to cause a rebellion, which would create problems with Rome. This spirit made Pilate and King Herod afraid that they would lose power and control. Making them feel that they had to eliminate Jesus and make him disappear.

If Jesus went through this, we should expect this and even more! They accused Jesus of being a false prophet, a terrorist, a riot instigator, a liar, a swindler, a charlatan, a sorcerer, a magician, Beelzebub, a sinner, a law breaker, a confused teacher, a confused interpreter of Torah, and a deceiver. If this spirit went to these lengths to discredit Jesus, what do you think it will do to you and me today?

Jesus said that He was going to the Father and would send the Holy Spirit to us so that we could do greater works than He had done. Satan is fighting us double-time. And he is succeeding in most churches. Where do you know that there is a church doing greater works than Jesus? This means that the principalities of darkness that are fighting us are winning. If we were doing more miracles than Jesus, I would say we were being victorious, but that is not the case. Satan has most churches in America sitting on "pause!" We are waiting for Jesus to come back and do these works. We are not seeking him. We have not consecrated ourselves, fasted, prayed, or tried to walk in the level of deliverance that the 12 disciples walked in daily.

The impact of the Jannes and Jambres' spirit on people:

It may be hard to imagine how Jannes and Jambres made an impact that turned Pharaoh's mind away from Moses' warning and the message from God. However, anyone can be deceived when opposition and manipulation are present. These were not ordinary circumstances that Moses and Aaron faced. They recognized that God was in charge and that the Holy Spirit was able to lead and guide them. This is how we should be each day of our Christian Walk.

The spirit that was possessing Jannes and Jambre WAS NOT from God. It was a "counterfeit spirit." We must watch for these types of spirits in the last days. These spirits have total control in the presence of unbeliever, especially when fear is present.

Jannes and Jambre would have presented before Pharaoh with their negative attitude, marked by sarcasm, towards Moses. They replicated Moses' "miracles," resulting in Moses' words being discredited before Pharaoh. Any time evil men or evil spirits discredit a man or woman of God in front of non-believers, it is easier for non-believers to be deceived.

Faith in God is what helps us avoid being deceived. Evil cannot be controlled or blocked without the guidance of the Holy Spirit. The non-believer (a non-saved person) does not possess the Holy Spirit to help them recognize the falsehoods of the evil spirits or false prophets. This results in them falling prey to these spirits or being "blinded" to the tricks of Satan.

When Moses and Aaron went before Pharaoh with a word from God, Satan became angry. He realized that his party was about to come to an end. The great "I am" had already provided Moses and Aaron with the "tools" or miracles to perform before Pharaoh. Under normal circumstances, without other evil interference, this would have worked. Pharaoh would have complied without questioning because Moses' miracles would have brought fear upon Pharaoh and his court members. However, with the interference of this evil spirit on Jannes and Jambre, Pharaoh's heart would harden each time after he had already accepted God's will and way.

However, when Pharaoh called for his magicians to ask their advice, they laughed and said that these were comment tricks—child's play! Satan knew that if they could replicate the miracles God had given Moses, then Pharaoh would not recognize it as a miracle from God but think of it as a cheap magician trick. If the devil cannot stop you from being blessed, anointed, or victorious, then his next best option is to try to discredit you. He will settle for convincing people that you are operating under the spirit of witchcraft and deceitfulness. Or that your anointing is fake.

Satan does not care what you do or how blessed you are; as long as he can diminish your influence on others, he is happy. Satan knew that he could not convince Pharaoh that there was a true God in heaven, so he chose the best option: to persuade Pharaoh that everything he saw was a cheap imitation or, at best, some fake magic.

The primary focus of a Jannes and Jambre spirit is opposition. The second side, or focus, is a behavior that attempts to discredit the true power of God and the genuine men and women of God. This spirit operates by appearing to tell the truth. This spirit will always have witnesses and act on behalf of or under the authority of a group that it has worked its way into deceitfully. This spirit never acts alone. It will infiltrate a group and ensnare all its members before launching an attack. It triggers and stimulates the situation that results in the catastrophic event, which is used as a catalyst to gain more control. Everyone thinks that this person is the savior of the group or church.

However, the true prophets of God and anointed pastors recognize this spirit and know that it is the true saboteur. This type of behavior is part of the third side of this spirit—making up the 'triple-agent" complex. Because this spirit always displays three sides and sometimes four, if necessary, to deceive everyone in the church or group.

Jannes and Jambres Are Examples of False Teachers:

Jannes and Jambre were false teachers, prophets, and magicians. The spirit of Jannes and Jambre is a spirit of opposition that excels due to its deception, false truths, and deceptive maneuvers. In II Timothy, the apostle Paul outlines how this spirit, the spirit of Antichrist, and the spirit of Jezebel, will run rampant in the last days.

In ***II Thessalonians 2,*** the Apostle Paul discusses the apostasy of Christians and the state of the church in the last days. As Paul outlines to

Timothy and the Thessalonians what will happen in the last days, one thing is certain—false teachings will occur. False prophets and the antichrist will try to deceive Christians. The message that is front and center in both of these books is the prevalence of false teachings and false prophets.

How to recognize the Spirit of Jannes and Jambre in your church:

This spirit is also known as the "false teacher" or "false prophet." The "false teacher/prophet spirit" often goes undetected in most churches because it is a master of deception. This spirit becomes empowered to deceive in a church by appearing to be "super" anointed. These individuals, under the control of this spirit, are master con artists, convincing the entire church and leadership team that they communicate directly with God and that He continually speaks to them.

The people under the influence of this spirit appear to be righteous and incredibly godly at all times. If you listen closely, you will find that they always discuss what God has said to them, what he is condemning, or what upsets God. You never hear them discussing personal spiritual growth—only the regurgitation of Old Testament Law, denominational legalism, or what they think the people of the church want to hear. Their conversations are always about whatever it takes to "suck" supporters into their group.

They have become such masters of godliness by appearing to be "super" anointed, and they claim to always have God's voice in their ears. We must not be deceived by these individuals who appear righteous and incredibly "godly." Still, we need to ensure that they do not deceive us, because they are skilled at defying the true power of God and discrediting anyone who has a genuine relationship with God or His Son, Jesus Christ.

Another way to recognize this spirit is to watch how it opposes those who are truly godly. They will continually discredit these godly pastors and all the truths that they speak about the word of God and the end times. This spirit is all about freedom and tolerance. Accepting everyone as they are, without trying to change them.

Last week, I had a praise and worship leader tell me, "Oh, Sis. La Wanda, the first thing you need to learn is that God made us, and he loves us. There is no way that God would change a thing about us. Then she began singing the song to me by Meagan Woods, "I was made in the image of a Perfect King!" She began to tell me that God made her in His image and that when He looks at her, He wouldn't change a thing. I am certain this was not the author's intention to support a gay lifestyle choice with her song. But this spirit had convinced her that, however God made her—no matter how wrong or sinful the Bible said it was—was okay because Megan Woods said that she was made in the image of a perfect king, and he wouldn't change a thing.

See how this spirit takes a scripture and lyrics and twists them to fit the woke agenda, justifying her choices? Well, this praise and worship leader was in a Pentecostal evangelical church, singing and praying in "tongues," trying to pray and sing down the power of God before the pastor got up to preach. This pastor claimed to be a "prophet" whom God had been speaking to lately.

> The truth is, I am my Father's child.
> **I make Him proud, and I make Him smile.**
> I was made in the image of a perfect King.
> **He looks at me and wouldn't change a thing.**
> The truth is, I am truly loved.
> By a God who's good when I'm not good enough
> I don't belong to the lies; I belong to You.
> And that's the truth.
>
> Song by Meagan Woods
> "Truth" 2024

I have posted the chorus here so that you can see the lyrics in writing. Sometimes, when we listen to a song on the radio, if it has a catchy beat or tune, we get caught up in the music and fail to pay attention to the lyrics. This is another way that demonic spirits can influence us. As Christians, we must be cautious. Since this gay praise and worship leader used this song, I want to address the lyrics and what is wrong with them. I usually refrain from criticizing other ministers or songwriters. However, I believe it is appropriate to address this issue at this time.

I have nothing against Meagan Woods. I am sure that her intent was pure when she wrote this song. But in the process of getting something catchy, with a popular tune, I think she allowed the Leviathan spirit to twist some words for her.

The first time I heard this song, I felt my blood stand still in my veins and my heart skip several beats. The cringe that shook my body was my spiritual alarm system going off. As soon as I got home, I went to my laptop and searched for the lyrics. I wanted to read them and ensure I was hearing what I thought I had heard.

Here are the problems with these lyrics as written. These problems are not because I think Meagan Woods is evil, but because I fear that Satan will use the lyrics to deceive our youth. Then last week, I had these lyrics quoted to me with the intent that I feared Satan would be using them.

1) We are made in the image of God.
2) Our Heavenly Father and his son, Jesus, who will be our Groom at the Marriage Supper and our King during the Millennial Reign, are perfect.
3) Yes, Jesus will be a perfect king
4) The heavenly Father cannot look upon us because of our sin, except we are covered in the blood of Jesus, the Lamb that took away our sins.
5) Therefore, God does not look at us and say he would not change a thing. That is a false concept. God looks at us through the blood of Jesus (which covers our sins). God sees our hearts. He sees things man does not. But God always wants us to be more Christ-like, not complacent in our Christian Walk.
6) Jesus frequently told his disciples to pray to be more like him. They were his chosen. They were so much closer to God than any of us could ever imagine. They were not perfect—just forgiven.
7) I feel that every time I kneel down to pray, I am humbled and honored to feel his presence in my war room. The spirit that I feel when I am there praying is the opposite of pride and haughtiness. When I am kneeling there, I always feel that there is more that I can do and that more rough edges that need to be filed off. I never feel justified to the point that I cannot improve. I realize that I am justified through the blood of Jesus Christ and that I do not have to be overwhelmed with condemnation, but I know that I am not perfect. There are days and times when I do not exhibit all of the fruits of the Spirit at the same time. Some days I struggle.
8) How can we sing that we do not need to change? We can always be better. We can always be closer to God. We can always have a stronger relationship with Jesus.

Jannes and Jambre knew that Moses' message to Pharaoh was a message of truth from God. Even though they were known in certain circles as the "Sons of Baal" (according to the scriptures in Exodus 8:18-19), they still recognized a power greater than their own. Yes, Satan can recognize the real power of God. That is what makes this spirit feel threatened and lash out in an attempt to control. We must ensure that this spirit or any other spirits do not deceive us.

> *Exodus 8:18-19—And the magicians did so with their enchantments to bring forth lice, but they could not: so, there were lice upon man, and beast. Then the magicians said unto Pharaoh, this is the finger of God: and Pharaoh's heart was hardened, and he hearkened not unto them, as the Lord had said.* (KJV, 2025).

You need to take the time to read the story of the exodus of the children of Israel from Egypt this week. Re-read the chapters that deal with the plagues and how Pharaoh responded to each plague. It was very intriguing to me how Pharaoh responded—how this spirit of opposition influenced him, etc. Pay close attention to the frogs everywhere. When asked when he wanted God to remove the frogs after he agreed to let the children of Israel go, Pharaoh responded, "Tomorrow!"

This response has always been alarming to me. I have always wondered, "Why on earth would anyone want to spend one more night with the frogs in their beds, food, and everywhere?" The spirit of opposition deceived the Pharaoh so much that he did not make sound decisions. Watch the actions of this spirit when it is operating in people's lives, especially church leadership staff. You will notice that they are making irrational decisions and acting as if that is normal. I call it the *"One More Night with the Frogs" Syndrome!*

The Goals of the "Spirit of Jannes and Jambres."

1) Deceive as many people as they can reach or influence.
2) Control all church events and services, keeping the real power of God from operating.
3) Convince everyone that the "fake truth" is real.

American Culture (non-religious) is an example of this spirit.

1) Beyoncé shared her demonic possession with pride to the world and how it had changed her life. She encouraged young people to let go and allow the spirit to take them, making it appear as easy and harmless as grabbing a slice of pizza from the box on the coffee table and eating it while crashing on the couch!
2) The influence of KISS—Kings in Satan's Service Music Group and the millions they reached and influenced during the 70s and 80s.
3) The impact of the LGBTQIA+ lie on equality and acceptance—woke culture.

Consequences of allowing yourself to be influenced by this spirit:

There will always be consequences for our actions and/or decisions. When examining the story of Simon, the Sorcerer, and his desire to possess the power of the Holy Ghost and the apostles' power through their anointing, it becomes clear that Simon, the Sorcerer, was consumed by his desires. Simon prioritized securing the apostles' power at any cost, disregarding the cost to himself. He did not care what it cost him; he did not care who he cheated or hurt as long as he got what he wanted—the power to elevate himself before everyone.

If Simon had been granted the apostles' power for a price, he would have used that power to heal people and deliver others. Of course, he would have charged a fee to each person. As a result of his newfound power, he would have become wealthy. This is never the purpose of the Holy Spirit. God never grants us an anointing or gift so that we can use it to become wealthy. God grants us our spiritual gift for several reasons.

The most important reason for God granting a person or preacher one of the gifts of the Spirit or a special anointing is for the edification of the church. This includes encouragement and uplifting one's spirits with words of prophecy that offer hope and inspiration. Edification can also include prophetic words that provide a congregation with something to strive for. On rare occasions, the word might be negative because the congregation has not obeyed God's directives.

The second reason God grants a gift, such as the gift of healing, to one person in a church is to build the faith of younger Christians who do not understand how faith works or how to put their faith into action. However, if they know that someone is used in the gift of healing, it is easier for them to believe that they can be healed. Faith is the key here—not the person.

The third reason God might grant a special gift, especially the gift of tongues with interpretation, to one person in a church is to have someone present through whom a direct message from God could come to the congregation. The Apostle Paul describes the main benefit of this spirit as "edification." When a message in tongues has been received and interpreted, it always encourages the person receiving it. Even if part of the message is a rebuke, it still encourages. Once the Holy Ghost has spoken, the individual knows when to move and what to do. Sometimes God has to get our attention.

I have experienced God speaking to me over the years through either a prophetic word or a message in tongues. In 2003, the Lord sent a prophetic word through an Evangelist that I had never met until that year. I had no idea that the next two and a half years of my life would be one of the toughest periods I would ever face. Many times, during that time frame, I would quote the prophetic words to the devil. That message, which would have appeared as nothing to most people, was the words that brought me through. Not that the man or the words had power, but those words kept my faith in God at the level I needed to receive what God had for me. It was a life-changing experience. One that put me in a place with my relationship with Jesus Christ that I had never known. Then, on top of that, the trial taught me to pray over everything and trust nothing until I had prayed and heard from God.

As you can see from these three examples, none of these individuals received any monetary reward or fame for obeying God. Today, it is easy for us to ask what a gift will do for us or bring to us. If it will not do anything for us, we are not interested. We are no different from Simon the Sorcerer if we feel this way. A gift from God is for us as individuals, but it is also for the church. Our gift might draw people to our church, but it is never to draw fame and fortune to us individually.

You may be questioning why I am sharing this and what this has to do with Jannes and Jambre. You need to be aware of how spirits work on all levels. Not every spirit you meet will be as advanced as the Spirit of Jannes and Jambre. It may be a smaller spirit or a spirit that is just beginning to operate in someone's life. Those are harder to recognize, especially if you know that person. Sometimes we pass off spirit manifestations as the person's nature or quirks. So, it is important that we learn how to recognize all levels of spirits.

God desires for us to be aware of what is happening around us in the spirit realm. God wants you to sit back and patiently wait on the Holy Spirit. He will reveal the ulterior motives of your opponents, colleagues, and fellow church members. God will even show you what your family is doing behind your back. It is incredible to me the lengths and depths people will go to be on top or have bragging rights, mainly among family and close friends.

When Satan is trying to lure you into his circle or deceive you with a false prophet, he never lets you see the consequences of making those choices. However, we know that every decision in life has consequences, some of which are beneficial, while others are detrimental. If you are fortunate, the consequences are neutral and non-damaging.

The only way to survive the consequences of actions like Simon's (the sorcerer) is to repent. Without true, accurate, heartfelt repentance, Simon would have perished. God would have killed him on the spot.

The only way to prevent falling prey to Satan's tricks and getting caught up in the selfish game is to examine your personal and spiritual lives continually. I strongly recommend reading **Jude 3, II Corinthians 9, and Acts 17** when you get a chance this week. You need to understand how to examine your life for any weak areas that allow Satan's strategies to work.

After completing those three chapters, read John 8 and I John 4 to prepare yourself to discern the truth from false information and to learn how to identify the spirits of those around you. **I John 4** instructs us to "test the spirits" so that we can recognize which information is from God and which is "fake truth" presented to us by Satan and his followers.

Other secular works that discuss Jannes and Jambre:

It is essential to understand that we can gain valuable insights into Jannes and Jambres and how their "sorcery" functioned, as well as how this spirit exploited them deceptively to oppose Moses and Aaron, by examining other historical records and secular books that provide information about them. I will not delve into details or quote these works. However, for the sake of transparency on this topic, I would like to share with you other public or secular works that include information on Jannes and Jambre, as well as the events that occurred in their lives before, during, and after their encounter with Moses and Aaron in Pharaoh's court.

Some theologians believe that the encounter of Jannes and Jambre in Pharaoh's court was not their only meeting with Moses and Aaron. According to information found in other secular works, Jannes and Jambre may have been persuaded by the miracles they could not replicate—the plagues—that struck Egypt, leading them to recognize the God of Heaven as the only true God. We know they recognized God's handiwork by their comments to Pharaoh, listed in Exodus.

If they truly believed as they said, there is a strong possibility that they went to Goshen and met with other Israelites. They may have had a private meeting with Moses and Aaron away from Pharaoh's court.

Some theologians believe that Jannes and Jambre may have accompanied the children of Israel out of Egypt. Some Jewish philosophers believe that these two individuals were present in the wilderness when the people urged Aaron to create a graven image (idol) for worship. Others believe that Jannes and Jambre would have been the only ones knowledgeable enough to instruct Aaron in making the calf and initiating the pagan worship that Moses found when he returned from the mountain with the Ten Commandments.

It seems plausible that this spirit was present and had an impact on the Israelites. Even if Jannes and Jambre did not leave Egypt with the Israelites. Even if Jannes and Jambre were not the teachers of idol-making to Aaron, the spirit of opposition, deception, and false truths was definitely present when Moses was on the mount. This spirit convinced the children of Israel that they needed a god that they could see, feel, and hear. Not an invisible God. A spirit can attach itself to someone when they are in the presence of a person who is possessed. The spirit that controlled Jannes and Jambre could have been in contact with someone in the Israeli camp at any point or time.

Therefore, it is reasonable to conclude that the spirit of Jannes and Jambre left Egypt with the children of Israel and influenced them during the entire 80-year trek through the wilderness. This spirit was still present when Joshua attempted to take possession of the land of Canaan. If you want to know more about this spirit of "selfishness" and how it lies to people, study the story of Achan and how he stole the garments and gold from Jericho.

Study the consequences that occurred to him and his family because of his sins. See how Satan deceived him into his actions. You can Google the following terms and search through these documents for more information, if desired, on Jannes and Jambre, as well as what the Jewish Talmud and other first- and second-century philosophers thought.

Jewish Targum of Jonathan
Jewish Talmud
Pliny the Elder (1st century AD)
Apuleius (2nd Century AD)
Neo-Platonist Numenius of Apamea (2nd Century AD)

Paul was a student of Gamaliel (**See Acts 22**). Gamaliel taught Paul about Moses, Jannes, and Jambre, which may have led to the inclusion of some Jewish scrolls, journals, books, or records that attest to the accuracy of the various Old Testament histories surrounding Moses and Aaron's confrontation with and opposition from Jannes and Jambre in Exodus.

We may not have all the details of what happened in Pharaoh's court in Egypt or what occurred in the wilderness with the idol worship. However, we can recognize the character traits of the spirits that were present, spirits that had influenced individuals in Egypt, and the spirits that were trying to stop the children of Israel from becoming a nation. We have seen these same spirits in operation throughout history—for example, the Holocaust, Jews in exile from numerous countries, ethnic cleansing attempts throughout history, and many instances of opposition to the spreading of the gospel of Jesus Christ.

Consider the numerous versions of churches that exist. Compare these with the various teachings of those churches, and debate the differences to determine what is true and what is insignificant. Only then will you realize the power of the spirit of opposition and deception in the world and how it continues to impact denominational churches today.

Watch Christian television (Daystar, TBN, Son Life Broadcasting, and other networks in your geographical area). You will notice numerous differences in the teachings if you listen to at least 10 hours a day for a week. One preacher will preach that once saved, you are always safe. He will declare this is what the New Testament says, and that Jesus taught this concept to his disciples, and that Paul shared this same doctrine with the churches at Corinth and Ephesus.

Then another preacher will come on, stating that there are no eternal guarantees. That we must daily bury our flesh and come under subjection to the Holy Spirit. I could go on for a hundred pages or more on the differences that you would hear on Christian television. With these controversial topics being discussed, it is clear how a spirit of confusion, controversy, and control can infiltrate the Christian community.

There are numerous questions that we will never know the answers to until we reach Heaven. With only 66 books or manuscripts selected of the 2000 plus manuscripts when King James commissioned the development of the Bible so that each man, woman, and child could have a Bible that they could carry with them and study, it is safe to say that we are missing a lot of the stories that could impact how we believe or feel.

Recognizing the limitations of my knowledge base, I daily thank God for the 66 books I have access to and ask Him to speak to me through His word, guiding me to daily change and become more Christ-like. Now, you understand why I always suggest further research and studies to help improve our walk with God. This also helps to explain why my spiritual man had such a reaction to Meagon Wood's song "*The Truth*" (2024).

Do not ever stop studying! Do not stop searching for the truth! Pray daily. Read your Bible daily. Spend quality time with God each day. Nurture your relationship with him as you would with your spouse or children. God loves us. We are made in his image—now act like it!

CHAPTER TWO:

Why did Jannes & Jambre oppose Moses?

In the Old Testament, Jannes and Jambre are mentioned as magicians in Pharaoh's court. Although their names are not listed in the book of Exodus, the Apostle Paul mentions them by name in his letter to Timothy. Let us examine the information about these magicians in Exodus and compare it with Paul's writings.

The strange case of Jannes and Jambres

For a minute, I was hoping you could look at this from a different perspective. Let's say you are preparing to preach or lead a Bible study on *II Timothy 3* when you come across Jannes and Jambres. Suddenly, you are bombarded with questions. Who are these two men? Are these two men or a husband-and-wife team? When did this event happen? Why did they oppose Moses? How is their opposition to Moses similar to ("just as") what the false teachers are doing in first-century Ephesus?

You search your Bible and cannot find them anywhere. You try a different translation and still cannot find them. You tried varying the spelling, but there were still no findings. Ah, well, you say to yourself, "Maybe I'll just skim over that verse and hope nobody notices." But all the time, you have this nagging feeling that you should not ignore his name or these facts.

Something keeps telling you there is more to this story. You are right. There is more to this story. There is clear evidence of a spirit of opposition that was powerful in ancient times, but is now a hundredfold more effective. Then, as you begin reading the story in Exodus and II Timothy, you are now convinced that these two men opposed the truth at all costs, regardless of the consequences.

After extensive research, I discovered that the names Jannes and Jambre appear in some literature from the Qumran community (the Dead Sea Scrolls), several other Jewish sources, and even the Latin language writers Pliny and Apuleius, this may not seem important to you; however, I wanted you to know that there are resources other than the Bible that name Jannes and Jambre as being sorcerers in Pharaoh's court during the time frame when Moses would have returned to Egypt to try to expedite the exodus of the Jews out into the wilderness to offer sacrifices to their God, the Lord God Jehovah, the "I Am."

Moses took his brother Aaron as his spokesperson when he went before Pharaoh due to Aaron's speech impediment. God instructed Moses to give Aaron specific instructions on what to do, and God promised to use Aaron to perform these miracles so that Pharaoh would recognize he was the one true God. Immediately, Moses and Aaron began working miracles and speaking plagues into existence. No matter what Pharaoh saw, he continued to harden his heart, his mind refusing to accept Moses' words or God's authority. The spirit of opposition was so strong that Pharaoh was more content with accepting the "fake truth" than the real truth.

When Pharaoh called for the magicians and Jannes and Jambres, they began replicating Aaron's miracles (see **Exodus 7**). These magicians or sorcerers could mimic the plagues of blood and frogs, but for some reason, they were defeated by gnats and lice (8:18) and were unable to do any further harm. For whatever reason, the gnats and lice were their downfall. They admitted to Pharaoh that these miracles were of the one true God. Had they changed? Had Moses and Aaron gotten to them?

They opposed Moses because it was more popular for them to be on Pharaoh's side and keep the children of Israel as slaves. It benefited Jannes and Jambres by promoting false teachings that benefited their benefactor, the Pharaoh. Often, our family and friends side against us because it pleases them, and at other times, because it brings them financial gain.

At no point do we have any indication that Jannes and Jambre stood with Moses and Aaron because it was the right thing ethically to do—no, they were concerned more about their health and wealth than the cruelty of slavery! This attitude is the prevailing condition among those who currently control the churches. Pastors, pastors' wives, and other pastoral staff are more concerned about what they are getting, what they have, and what they can manipulate out of the congregation than what aligns with the word of God. For your convenience, I have included the seventh chapter of Exodus here for you to read.

> **EXODUS 7:8-18**—*"And the LORD spake unto Moses and unto Aaron, saying, When Pharaoh shall speak unto you, saying, Shew a miracle for you: then thou shalt say unto Aaron, Take thy rod, and cast it before Pharaoh, and it shall become a serpent. And Moses and Aaron went in unto Pharaoh, and they did so as the LORD had commanded: and Aaron cast down his rod before Pharaoh, and before his servants, and it became a serpent. Then Pharaoh also called the wise men and the sorcerers: now the magicians of Egypt, they also did in like manner with their enchantments. For they cast down every man his rod, and they became serpents: but Aaron's rod swallowed up their rods.*
>
> *And he hardened Pharaoh's heart, that he hearkened not unto them; as the LORD had said. And the LORD said unto Moses, Pharaoh's heart is hardened, he refuseth to let the people go. Get thee unto Pharaoh in the morning; lo, he goeth out unto the water; and thou shalt stand by the river's brink against he comes, and the rod which was turned to a serpent shalt thou take in thine hand. And thou shalt say unto him, The LORD God of the Hebrews hath sent me unto thee, saying, let my people go, that they may serve me in the wilderness: and, behold, hitherto thou wouldest not hear. Thus, saith the Lord, "In this thou shalt know that I am the Lord: behold, I will smite with the rod that is in mine hand upon the waters which are in the river, and they shall be turned to blood.*
>
> *And the fish that is in the river shall die, and the river shall stink, and the Egyptians shall loathe to drink of the water of the river. And the LORD spake unto Moses, say unto Aaron, "Take thy rod, and stretch out thine hand upon the waters of Egypt, upon their streams, upon their rivers, and upon their ponds, and upon all their pools of water, that they may become blood; and that there may be blood throughout all the land of Egypt, both in vessels of wood, and in vessels of stone."*

> *And Moses and Aaron did so, as the LORD commanded; and he lifted up the rod, and smote the waters that were in the river, in the sight of Pharaoh, and in the sight of his servants; and all the waters that were in the river were turned to blood. And the fish that was in the river died; and the river stank, and the Egyptians could not drink of the water of the river; and there was blood throughout all the land of Egypt.*
>
> *And the magicians of Egypt did so with their enchantments: and Pharaoh's heart was hardened, neither did he hearken unto them; as the LORD had said. And Pharaoh turned and went into his house, neither did he set his heart to this also. And all the Egyptians digged round about the river for water to drink; for they could not drink of the river's water. And seven days were fulfilled, after that the LORD had smitten the river.* (KJV, 2024).

Before I begin discussing Jannes and Jambres' opposition to Moses, let us read the scriptures about the plagues that God sent on Egypt because Pharaoh kept hardening his heart and changing his mind about allowing the children of Israel to go into the wilderness to worship God and offer sacrifices to him. To understand the alleged change of heart of Jannes and Jambre and how they impacted Pharaoh's decision about letting the children of Israel go, you need to hear about the plagues and look at which ones Jannes and Jambre were able to duplicate.

Now the Plagues—Exodus 8:1-10

> **EXODUS 8:1-10**: *And the LORD spake unto Moses, Go unto Pharaoh, and say unto him, thus saith the LORD, let my people go, that they may serve me. And if thou refuse to let them go, behold, I will smite all thy borders with frogs: And the river shall bring forth frogs abundantly,*

> which shall go up and come into thine house, and into thy bed-chamber, and upon thy bed, and into the house of thy servants, and upon thy people, and into thine ovens, and into thy kneading troughs: And the frogs shall come up both on thee, and upon thy people, and upon all thy servants.
>
> And the LORD spake unto Moses, say unto Aaron, Stretch forth thine hand with thy rod over the streams, over the rivers, and over the ponds, and cause frogs to come up upon the land of Egypt. And Aaron stretched out his hand over the waters of Egypt; and the frogs came up, and covered the land of Egypt. And the magicians did so with their enchantments and brought up frogs upon the land of Egypt.
>
> Then Pharaoh called for Moses and Aaron, and said, Intreat the LORD, that he may take away the frogs from me, and from my people; and I will let the people go, that they may do sacrifice unto the LORD. And Moses said unto Pharaoh, Glory over me: when shall I entreat for thee, and for thy servants, and for thy people, to destroy the frogs from thee and thy houses, that they may remain in the river only? And he said, Tomorrow. And he said, be it according to thy word: that thou mayest know that there is none like unto the LORD our God.
> (KJV, 2024).

This is the final segment of scripture that I want us to read today. This passage is from the 8th chapter of Exodus. It will help you to see when the change began to occur in Jannes and Jambre. Once you read this passage, you will realize how this spirit "turned over the leaf" because it needed to know that it was on the winning team, regardless of which way this situation ended. If Pharaoh was victorious, they would be right there in Pharaoh's court. However, if the God of the Israelites won, they wanted to ensure that Moses and Aaron knew they recognized the God of Heaven as the one and only true God. I call this acquiring insurance, not assurance!

The southern term for this is "hedging their bet!" However, nowhere in Moses' writings or the writings of the Apostle Paul do we find a recorded conversion to the Jewish faith.

The Final Analysis of God's Miracles by Jannes and Jambre

> **EXODUS 8:16-19**: *And the LORD said unto Moses, say unto Aaron, stretch out thy rod, and smite the dust of the land, that it may become lice throughout all the land of Egypt. And they did so; for Aaron stretched out his hand with his rod, and smote the dust of the earth, and it became lice in man, and in beast; all the dust of the land became lice throughout all the land of Egypt. And the magicians did so with their enchantments to bring forth lice, but they could not: so, there were lice upon man and beast. Then the magicians said unto Pharaoh, this is the finger of God: Pharaoh's heart was hardened, and he hearkened not unto them, as the LORD had said.* (KJV, 2024).

The magicians said, *"This IS the finger of God: and Pharaoh's heart was hardened, and he hearkened not unto them; as the Lord had said."* (Exodus 8:19, KJV, 2024). It appears that turning the dust into gnats or lice was the first miracle they could not duplicate. At this point, it appears from Moses' writings that Jannes and Jambre recognized that the finger or hand of God was responsible for this miracle.

At this point, they realized the limitations of their magical powers and sorcery. They had been able to "counterfeit" the miracles up to this point. With God and his powers, there are no limits. But the scriptures tell us that God has set limits on Satan and his powers. Satan wants you to believe that he can do all things here on earth. But that is not entirely true. God has set limits on Satan and requires Satan to ask for permission to perform specific tasks.

Remember the story of Job and how Satan told God that he could not touch Job because God had a hedge around him. Satan wanted God to remove the hedge so that he could touch Job physically and take his health away. Satan told God that because of this hedge around Job, Job would always be grateful to God. However, Satan felt that if God would allow Satan the power to touch Job's health, Job would curse God and give up the ghost and die. Satan felt confident in his powers' ability to enact them as he saw fit. So, God allowed Satan to tempt Job. But Satan got the surprise of his life! Job was faithful to the end!

I can imagine the conversation between Jannes and Jambre when they realized they had reached the point where their magic failed to prove God wrong or deceive Pharaoh with a "fake truth." They had duplicated "counterfeit miracles" for so long and deceived many, including Pharaoh. But Satan's power only goes so far. Some miracles cannot be duplicated by fake anointing, sorcery, witchcraft, etc.

Now we need to examine the lengthy message the Apostle Paul gave to Timothy about the spirit of Jannes and Jambres, along with his recommendations or advice on how Timothy should handle the situation at Ephesus.

> **II Timothy 3:1-14**—*This knows also that in the last days, perilous times shall-come. For men shall be lovers of their own selves, covetous, boasters, proud, blasphemers, disobedient to parents, unthankful, unholy, without natural affection, trucebreakers, false accusers, incontinent, fierce, despisers of those that are good, traitors, heady, high-minded, lovers of pleasures more than lovers of God; having a form of godliness, but denying the power thereof: from such turn away. For of this sort are they which creep into houses and lead captive silly women laden with sins, led away with divers lusts, ever learning, and never able to come to the knowledge of the truth. As Jannes and Jambres withstood Moses, so do these also resist the truth: men of corrupt minds reprobate concerning the faith. But they shall proceed no further: for their folly shall manifest unto all men, as theirs was. But thou hast fully known my doctrine, manner of life, purpose, faith, longsuffering, charity, patience, Persecutions, afflictions, which came unto me at Antioch, at Iconium, at Lystra; what persecutions I endured: but out of them all the Lord delivered me. Yea, and all that will live godly in Christ Jesus shall suffer persecution. But evil men and seducers shall wax worse and worse, deceiving and being deceived. But continue thou in the things which thou hast learned and hast been assured of, knowing of whom thou hast learned them;* (JKV, 2024).

In the New Testament, the Jewish rabbinic scholar, the Apostle Paul, was trained under Gamaliel in the Jerusalem Temple. Gamaliel was a scholar and was regarded as one of the greatest interpreters of Jewish law and customs. I am certain that Gamaliel had studied the teachings and actions of Jannes and Jambres, as well as those of other sorcerers of that day.

This knowledge becomes evident in the Apostle Paul's writings to Timothy, particularly in the second letter of instruction he sent to him and the church at Ephesus. When Paul was teaching Timothy, he sought to impart some of the knowledge he had acquired from Gamaliel. Paul mentioned the opposing spirits that tried to discredit Moses and Aaron before Pharaoh and named them. This scripture in II Timothy provides us with their names. These names match other secular writings.

I have found two literary sources that I will mention here, not because they alter the facts of this story or book, but to provide additional scholarly information for readers who enjoy seeking out such information.

Albert Pietersma has noted in the *Anchor Bible Dictionary* (1992) that the two names "appear frequently in Jewish, Christian, and pagan sources extant in Arabic, Aramaic, Greek, Hebrew, Latin, Old and Middle English, and Syriac." (Vol. 3, p. 638).

Why the opposition?

In Exodus, we find the story of Moses returning to Egypt after 40 years of exile in the wilderness near Mount Sinai. Moses had been raised in Pharoah's court from infancy until he killed the Egyptian taskmaster who was beating the Israelite slave. Moses was familiar with the court's rules and the laws of God. Moses' mother, Jochebed, had taught him both ways as she "nursed" him for the Egyptian princess.

We do not have definitive evidence to provide a detailed genealogy of the Princess's family and Moses's adoptive cousins. However, there is a strong chance that the Pharaoh Moses stood before was his childhood friend during his formative years.

If Pharoah had grown up with Moses, he would have been skeptical from the beginning about Moses having any special powers or being anointed by God. Add to that the fact that magicians recreated the "miracles" that Moses was performing, and you can see why Pharaoh kept changing his mind about whether to lead the children of Israel into the wilderness to worship their God or not.

In defense of Jannes and Jambre embarking on a path to discredit Moses would have appeared normal, even to us today, if we had been raised in a country where a particular ethnic group had been the "slaves" of the

Pharaoh or king, like the Israelites had been in bondage for over 400 years to the Egyptians.

Now, place yourself in the shoes of Jannes and Jambres. Imagine you are a member of the board of directors of your church. You and your spouse are the pastor's two most trusted board members. Imagine that the pastor comes to you with all his issues and concerns, and depends on the two of you to ensure that no group or individual deceives him. Then imagine two men walking into your church on a Sunday, dressed like 1960s hippies, with long hair, rags for clothes, worn skin, long beards, thin hair with bald spots, speaking broken English with a very strong Southern redneck accent. What would be your first reaction? How would you move forward to protect your pastor? This is how I see Jannes and Jambre reacting to Moses and Aaron on that first trip to Pharaoh's court.

Jannes and Jambre moved into full "opposition mode" immediately. They had to protect Pharaoh from being deceived. They also had to protect their positions in the court. They could not allow Pharaoh to realize that there were two men more anointed and more powerful than they were in the kingdom. They had two immediate motives: protecting their king and country, as well as themselves. There is no greater motivator for someone to discredit another individual than the fear of losing their position, power, and influence.

We have limited information about Jannes and Jambres in the Old Testament outside of this story, where they are mentioned as magicians in Pharaoh's court. The Old Testament does not even list their names. However, Paul's letter to Timothy lists their names as Jannes and Jambre— **II Timothy 3:8** (JKV), as he retells this story from Exodus to Timothy. As we searched through Jewish literature, we found mention of Jannes and Jambre in several religious and secular literary works.

As we discuss this spirit and how it worked in the New Testament, we will also examine other literary works that validate the story of Moses and Aaron, including those of Jannes and Jambres. Several sources validate this information. The first was when they opposed Moses, and the second was when they joined them in the exodus.

Hopefully, discussing these facts will help you understand this spirit and how the Leviathan and Python spirits control it in so many churches. I do not have time to discuss the demonology of the Old Testament or how the ancient spirits worked then, compared to the New Testament. However, I would like to refer you to a book by Charlie O'Neal (2019) titled "***A Word from God for the Church.***" Charlie O'Neal also wrote a book (2020) titled "***Why am I not living a victorious life?***" Both books discuss various types of demons and their roles within the church and among individuals.

O'Neal shares how to recognize these demons, how to pray for deliverance, and whether you should leave a church where these spirits operate in the leadership team and board. When you finish this book, I strongly recommend reading these two books if you recognize any spirits controlling your church or your spiritual life.

The primary or controlling demons operating through Jannes and Jambre were the spirits of opposition, deception, and false prophecy. The latter, the spirit of false prophecy, is the main controlling spirit trying to destroy churches across America. Satan wants to discredit pastors just enough to keep people away from church. He aims to create "reasonable doubt" in the minds of potential and lukewarm church members, making them less committed to the church.

Jannes and Jambre did not recreate all of Moses and Aaron's miracles; they replicated some of them along with some of the plagues. It was just enough to discredit or create doubt in the minds of those who had not yet decided. Satan hopes that if he creates enough gossip or rumors opposing the truth of God's servants or anointed ones, they will convince the spiritually weak or undecided to accept the false doctrine as the truth.

When Pharaoh summoned Jannes and Jambres to his court, he wanted them to discredit Moses and Aaron or prove they were not from God or that their God was not real. Any time a king was presented with a situation or a group of people, they did not know whether to believe or not; they would use their "wise men" to prove or discredit the presenters, thereby controlling their power over the people.

Jannes and Jambre "copied" the miracles God had told Aaron to perform before Pharaoh, as if they were cheap tricks. Jannes and Jambre also recreated some of the plagues, such as the river of blood, bringing the frogs out of the Nile, and turning the dust into gnats or lice. Each time Jannes and Jambre could "copycat" a plague, Pharaoh would change his mind and send word to Moses and Aaron that he would not let the Israelites leave Egypt.

The Apostle Paul was aware of the power of "false prophets" and the impact they could have on young church leaders and converts. He warned Timothy to guard against "false prophets and teachers continually." Paul understood the power of the spirit of opposition and how it was used to deceive people. Paul had used his position, education, and power to control people in the temple at Jerusalem. Paul's power and his passionate dedication to make everyone believe as he did that drove him to hunt down the Christians in Jerusalem and Damascus, imprisoning and killing many of them.

Paul's opposing spirit did not operate through magic tricks like Jannes and Jambres. They were the copycat version of how this spirit operates. I have often wondered how Jannes and Jambres must have felt when they duplicated Moses' act of throwing the staff down and letting it become a snake, only to have their snakes eaten by Moses'. If we are observant, we can recognize this spirit because it may demonstrate some of the Christian traits and Holy Ghost power, but it cannot duplicate "all actions" of the Holy Spirit.

Why do we oppose God's will today?

It is easy to oppose things that we do not understand. It is even easier to fight against the preachers, teachers, and others in our lives and churches who we feel are wrong. Something in our genetic makeup makes us feel we must be the fighters and support the underdog. So, if someone is wrong and they are influencing others, we think we must join the fight and correct the misinformation network!

Satan knows this is one of our greatest human flaws—correcting things! So, Satan utilizes this as one of his most powerful tools against us. He convinces us that we MUST set the record straight. We must ensure that everyone knows the truth. He will convince you that you are responsible for ensuring everyone has the "truth or facts" and can make an informed decision.

I hate to disappoint you, but God DOES NOT need you to straighten anything out! God does not require you to retrain everyone and ensure everyone understands the truth of the matter. You and I are only responsible for what God has instructed us to do, say, preach, or teach. We are to give the word when the anointing comes on us or the Holy Spirit witnesses. As for the daily grind of calling everyone on the phone and ensuring they know the "truth" as you see it—that is NOT your job! If Satan has convinced you that this is what you are to do, then you need to find an altar, repent, and ask God to show you what you are to do and say and when. Then follow God's directions, and do not let the oppressing and opposing spirits of Jannes and Jambre get you all tied up in everybody's business and in church business that you are not privy to in the first place!

Sometimes we oppose God's anointing and do not even realize that Satan has lured us into that trap. Sometimes, we let family and friends convince us that we need to be involved when we do not. If more people spent more time with God, reading and praying, instead of talking on the phone or scrolling through Facebook, we would find that our churches have more anointing and that people would be drawn to our churches instead of being repelled by them.

Why do others oppose God's will and try to stop us?

The main reason is that they have been deceived and convinced that a "fake truth" is true. Satan is a master at securing the one person who can change your mind about an event or a person. Satan will use that person to get you into a frame of mind where you feel that it is your God-given calling to handle a situation and correct someone's ways, when, in reality, it is none of your business.

I find that most Christians who oppose the man or woman of God in their church are not even aware that they are opposing them. They have been deceived by the person operating under the influence of the spirit of Jannes and Jambres, or the spirit of Jezebel and Athalia (both are retaliating and jealous spirits).

We must learn to recognize these opposing spirits and then disregard them. When we ignore them, they lose fuel, and their fire eventually dies. Conversely, when we give credence to them by trying to correct or clarify the "truth," we inadvertently give them credit and power. This results in them becoming more powerful and presenting a greater opposition to what is right.

When do we see this spirit manifest itself most?

There are two specific times when this spirit manifests itself, even in the most spiritually grounded churches. This spirit is always present in family-started and controlled churches. It does not have to be a spirit on the church's leadership team. It can be present in anyone in the church. This spirit can lie dormant for years before reemerging. At other times, this spirit can be in control from the very beginning of a church's existence, without anyone recognizing its behind-the-scenes manipulation until a crisis occurs or the church splits.

Any time there is a need for someone to protect their position in the church, this spirit can flare up. It is part of human nature to be territorial and protective of one's life and family. This basic human instinct is very active in most churches. Especially when a family or two start a church, and they are there from conception through all the tough times. These individuals and families may try to secure church positions for their children and grandchildren. In most cases, there is no consideration for the "collateral damage" that occurs to other families and members. Their chief goal is to protect their positions at all costs. This spirit of Jannes and Jambre is a master in this type of warfare. These two magicians were determined to prevent Moses and Aaron from influencing Pharaoh. They did not want to lose their elite positions and benefits.

The second time this spirit rises in churches is when a group of individuals or a family feels the need to control all aspects of the church, especially its operations and the congregation's beliefs. **For example,** a church that has always been conservative and non-denominational fundamental Baptist, and a charismatic group begins attending. This new group is introducing concepts of spiritual warfare and new musical styles. They start to share with others in the church how to fast, pray, and travail in the spirit. Their evangelistic worship style is gaining popularity among the younger members. When incidents like this occur and individuals or pastors begin to feel that their power is limited or they are losing control, this spirit will show up. This spirit loves to discredit the newcomers.

La Wanda Blackmon

CHAPTER THREE:

What is the spirit of Jannes and Jambre?

    The spirit of Jannes and Jambre is ultimately a "spirit of opposition." It is based on deception, achieved by discrediting a true man or woman of God, altering enough of the truth to create a counterfeit that many would accept without investigation or questioning.

    As I researched a story or example of current-day deception to share with you in this book, helping you understand how this spirit infiltrates the church and is ultimately destroyed from the inside out, I was at a loss for a story that would not result in the total disintegration of another ministry.

    I am confident that everyone reading this book has heard of a minister, pastor, or church ministry devastated by the sinful actions of leaders and founders. Everywhere I looked, I found stories. However, I did not want this book to be a "ministry" bashing book, even if all of these examples covered a layer of deception that this spirit uses.

    Then I received my copy of the third book in the Charlie O'Neal "Victorious Living" series, "***The Spiritual Warrior***" (2021). The book's introduction tells the story of a dream Charlie O'Neal had—God gave him a vision to help explain what would happen in the last days before the rapture took place.

    Considering that we are living in those last days and evil has been unleashed upon America from 2008 to 2024 with such fervor that it is hard even to realize that this much evil could take control of one country in such a short period, I feel that Charlie O'Neal's dream/story is the perfect example for me to share.

Make sure to read the story thoroughly. Do not skip any parts. As you read this story, I want you to remember the two letters to Timothy from the Apostle Paul. You will see every aspect of the false teacher/preacher listed, including the spirit of Jezebel, Leviathan, Python, and Spiritual Witchcraft, as well as the false prophet and spirit of opposition presented in this story, represented by Jannes and Jambres.

First Church of God of Babylon

This is an excerpt from **"The Spiritual Warrior"** *by Charlie O'Neal (2021). It has been reprinted with written permission from Charlie O'Neal and HFT Publishing, Inc. (December 2023 release to Heritage House Foundation and Ministry, and La Wanda Blackmon, for use as a direct quote in this book and a book on Revelation). Permission was also received to create a handout of this excerpt for use* in a spiritual warfare course.

This information is a direct quote *from Charlie O'Neal's introduction to "The Spiritual Warrior"* (2021), with all paragraph formatting intact.

As God gave me the information for this book, I began praying for a dynamic opening chapter to help people realize that this book about being a "spiritual warrior" was not like the other 900+ books on the market. As I began to fast and pray because I felt my book was missing something critical, the Lord began to drop "GOD ideas and topics" into my mind each day.

After a few weeks, I decided to sit down and outline this list of ideas. When I read back over my outline, my brain went into orbit. I could hear the Holy Spirit speaking this story to me. My outline became a story about the "current state of affairs" of the evangelical churches in America. To make this story relatable, I have referred to it as the First Church of God in Babylon. This is in no way indicative of the USA denomination known as the Church of God or the Church of God in Christ. This story describes lots of churches in America.

I realize that most churches have only one of the conditions mentioned. I do not think you will find all of these conditions or programs in one church, but trust me, Satan wants every evangelical church to be like the one I describe in my story below. Read on, and enjoy. I will cover all the points of this story and help you avoid a similar situation from happening to you personally. I pray that pastors WORLDWIDE will read this book, take it seriously, and implement the measures I describe to prevent this from happening in their churches. Wake up, America! We do not want to be the Church of Babylon that Revelation talks about!

> *Good morning!*
>
> *Welcome to the First Church of God in Babylon!*
>
> *We are so happy to have you visiting us today. We welcome everyone to join us in worship. We know you will have a wonderful experience here because we have something for every age group and ethnic background. Our ushers will hand out "visitor packets" in a few minutes. When they come by your aisle, raise your hand, and they will give you one. Complete the contact card and place it in the offering bag when the usher brings it back at the end of our service's praise and worship.*
>
> *As we share with you the joy we feel in worshipping God, we want you to understand that we have worked very hard to perfect our church as much as is possible in this earthly realm. The Lord sent us a dear prophetess who has helped us realize our mission, vision, and goals. She has helped us make the needed changes to make everyone happy here. We are grateful to Prophetess Sister Jezebel and the prophets who followed her. Prophetess Jezebel has taught us that we do not have to be bound by legalism, rules, regulations, or the rituals of worship that we have all been taught.*
>
> *With the help of Prophetess Jezebel, we have discovered that our ancestors did not fully understand the concept of grace and how freely it is given to us. We want to ensure that you do not have to worry about sin and repentance all the time here. We will not judge you or make you feel guilty about the sins you commit.*
>
> *For those of you who visited while the former pastors were in charge here, we apologize that you often heard about hell and the rapture. Thanks for giving us a new chance to win you*

back. We no longer preach about hell. We do not scare our young people with talks about the rapture. Instead, we believe in providing uplifting sermons that help motivate you to be a "better you." You do not have to worry; our new, progressive, tolerant church is here to stay!

We will never return to the legalism or bondage of the older generations. We are free, and you will be happy, loved, and motivated here with us! We are the apple of God's eye and the light to the world around us. Our new leadership team is non-judgmental and strictly enforces our policies of equality, tolerance, love, and respect for all. We no longer preach on sin or give altar calls, as it is not necessary to scare people into committing to God. We just "love" people to God. They do not even have to accept Jesus as the son of God, either.

We have learned that we all worship the same invisible god. How or through whom we reach him is unimportant—only that we worship God! The First Church of God in Babylon is a church that excels in its evangelism, outreach ministries, home missions, foreign missions, and youth programs, surpassing the effectiveness of most churches. Because of this effectiveness, we are a less stressful church that definitely helps our members decrease their fear of punishment and relax. This process allows them to transition into a better, calmer, more productive version of themselves!"

If you are wondering if God endorsed these changes, know that we fasted and prayed about the future of our church. We believe that God sent Prophetess Jezebel and her prophetic team to us. She arrived when we began fasting and praying over these issues. God used her to show us that our church needed to be a non-hostile work and worship center.

We still teach that people need faith in God. We believe that God can heal and work miracles, and we have witnessed many such miracles here. We also know that God wanted us to implement the changes that Prophetess Jezebel recommended, because our membership began to increase as soon as we began the process.

This year, we have seen our numbers grow faster and larger than ever imagined. Our offerings have quadrupled. We now have a sports center and various types of buildings on our campus, offering programs for youth. It is incredible how much growth and spiritual freedom we began to feel after we sent the older members with their outdated church leaders to the nursing home. Their legalistic view and rules drove our young people away and deterred new members from joining us.

Prophetess Jezebel has also taught us that we should be a tree that bends when the winds of trials come, so we will not break. We do not need to stand firm on convictions and bend, break, or fall apart. As a beautiful bending tree, we can provide endless beauty to God and the community for years to come!

There is no need for Daniel, Shadrack, Meshack, and Abednego, or people like them, in our church at the First Church of God in Babylon. We do not need their drama or the "words from god" they are always prophesying. They never have uplifting words—just woes, instructions to change, and all this nonsense about "choosing whom you will serve—choose whether you are going to be on God's side!"

We are all on God's side here—all paths lead to heaven now. We know that God understands that if we bend, bow down, compromise, or do whatever is necessary to fit in within our communities. There is no need for fear of compromising. God wants us to change with the culture and adapt to the next generation. If not, we will lose the next generation, their labor, and their money! We now incorporate technology into everything we do at The First Church of God in Babylon!

Technology enables us to reach a much larger audience. We tell them to come as they are—no need to change at all! Come here, and we will help you sit back, relax, and be entertained by our technology and programs. We will rock your souls to sleep spiritually as we decrease your worry about hell and the rapture!

We want you to understand that God has and always will give us plenty of warning before time runs out for us or the end comes. God is a god of love, grace, and mercy. He created us. We are his children. Just like you, God would never send his children to hell or kill them! You have nothing to worry about.

You will have plenty of time before you die to correct your sins and ask for forgiveness. God does not expect you to be perfect. He knows that you are human and will sin a little each day. That is why he is so merciful. To maintain His mercy on *your side, all you need to do is love God and attend church. If you do good work, read your Bible, and pray each day, then that helps God love you even more.*

Remember, God will never send you to hell as long as you believe in him and love him, regardless of what you do! Oh my, no, you will never have to worry about anyone judging you here at The First Church of God in Babylon for any sexual pleasures that you might engage in each day. God is love. He made us, and he created sex for our pleasure. Why would he create something and tell us we could not enjoy it? God made each one of us unique and special. He could never judge us for our indiscretions or alternative lifestyle desires. He made us this way!

Here at the First Church of God in Babylon, we no longer tolerate the lies that are spread around by those Pentecostals down the street. They claim that adultery, fornication, bestiality, sodomy, any lust, abortion, illegal drugs, and alcohol will not enter heaven. They tell you that queer, transgender, homosexuals, lesbians, and gays embracing alternate lifestyle choices will burn in hell because they are part of the "works of the flesh" that God has condemned from entering heaven.

But here, we embrace the LGBTQIA+ community with open arms. We know God loves them—he made them. We know He uses them and will continue to use them because they have chosen to love and serve Him. If God made them this way, how can He turn them away from heaven? They are his creation. We believe God wants us to welcome all and not worry about what they do.

If God wants them to change, he will lead them to change. We believe that God is all about balance and acceptance. Even in the gospels, Jesus never condemned those involved in sexual pleasure positions or those who enjoyed sexual perversions. You will never find the words transgender, homosexual, or lesbian in the Bible! You will not find these words because it is okay to participate. We did not understand this until Prophetess Jezebel led the revival here last year, which marked the beginning of our church's transformation. God so graciously gave us this chance to change and grow!

There is a balance here in all things at The First Church of God in Babylon. We accept all religions and faiths, regardless of one's beliefs. We believe that all paths lead to God, even those that do not accept Jesus Christ as the Son of God. As long as they do not hate Jesus, it will not matter whether we accept him or not. He is just the son, not God himself! We have realized that getting caught up in the drama of defending our faith to the point of saying that Jesus is the only way is no longer necessary! We must live a balanced and compassionate life, secure in the knowledge that a loving God has us all in His hands every day.

We offer vibrant and emotionally charged praise and worship services here. We take pride in our entertainment and the online reviews we receive for our services and outreach efforts. We are so proud of our prayerless pulpits, services without altar calls, and the dramas we put on for our youth. We believe our stage should be kept simple, without cluttering it with church furniture, communion tables, and altars.

We require all the floor space on and around the stage for our musical instruments, technology (especially our multiple 100-foot flat screens, which are integrated to rival those of a theater), and dancers. We believe that entertaining our young people every week is what God expects us to do. It is better for them to be entertained here than in a local bar or nightclub. At least they are in church!

We also offer a singing-only Sunday for the adults. They can come to church and listen to gospel music for hours without worrying about anyone preaching to them. We are proud to say that we feel that the more parties, events, dinners, rodeos, camps, beach trips, movies, sports events, Disney World trips, canoeing, and offering sports events or worldly pleasures to our young people, we can make it easier for them to stay involved in the church and secure its future for the next generation.

We hope you stopped by our coffee bar and bookstore on your way in today. We strongly encourage you to stop by for a cup of coffee and a snack if you have not done so. Then, proceed to the mezzanine on the second floor and spend time in fellowship with your fellow church members. This building, the sports center, the gym, the coffee bar, and the mezzanine are open all day on

> *Saturdays and Sundays, and from 4 pm to midnight each night during the week.*
>
> *Thanks so much for joining us today at The First Church of God in Babylon! We have something here for everyone and hope you will return and make this your home church. Next Sunday, you can drop your suggestions for entertainment and programs in the suggestion box or the offering bags during the service. Your suggestions are vital to us and will help us plan events you enjoy.*
>
> *We are organizing a motorcycle rally next month and have just booked a race car driver to put on a show for our teenagers in two weeks. We are so excited. Sign up for these events at the front entrance information center.*
>
> *Remember, we are about love, tolerance, balance, and spiritual fulfillment, as we help you sit back, relax, and be entertained. We want you to feel supported, not stressed, and not to complain or feel trapped. We want to help you go with the flow spiritually so you can be a fulfilled and happy Christian.*
>
> **See you next Sunday!**
>
> Multiple reprints and use granted by permission of HFT Publishing, Inc., Brewton, AL (2021-2026).

This story of the First Church of God in Babylon effectively conveys the teachings of the Apostle Paul in II Timothy, Paul's admonitions to the Thessalonians in II Thessalonians, and the teachings of the Apostle John in the Book of Revelation regarding the spirit of Babylon and Jezebel. I realize this story is "fictional." However, everything in this story I have seen in churches across America.

I have not witnessed all of these incidents and details in one church, but I have been in churches where three or more of these things were operating simultaneously. Remarkably, I have found a pastor in denial each time I have noticed several of these events in a single church. When I have pointed out to these pastors the controlling spirits, the discrepancies, and the "twisting" of the truth, they always go into "protective mode" and try to explain away why those individuals are involved in the actions I have noted.

Let me tell you—we do not need excuse makers—we need truth teachers in our churches today! We need people willing to speak the truth, regardless of who is offended or stops attending our church. We should not fear the largest tithe payers and most influential members; instead, we should focus on pleasing God, rather than addressing opposing spirits within our churches.

The spirit of Jannes and Jambre should never be tolerated in our churches. Their opposition is there for one reason—to deceive the membership—and destroy the church! God has sent us with a purpose—deliverance! God wants us to lead his children from bondage to victory. We may not be facing slavery like the children of Israel, but Satan has most churches in so much bondage that slavery would be freedom! We must teach our members that there is victory in Jesus—consistently—every day—no exceptions. Put on the whole armor of God and seek God's will through prayer, fasting, and reading his word. The answer is there for us.

Stand today and resist Satan and his opposing magicians. Stand on God's word firmly—do not let family and friends stop you. Do not waver on what God has instructed you to do. If your destiny appears on hold, seek God and find out why. Has God applied the brakes, trying to give you time to recognize what you are dealing with, or has God allowed the opposition to stop you like Job, so he can slow you down and talk to you?

Let us examine **II Timothy 3:7-9** and what the Apostle Paul had to say about Jannes and Jambres.

II Timothy 3:7-9—*"Ever learning, and never able to come to the knowledge of the truth. Now, as Jannes and Jambres withstood Moses, so do these also resist the truth: men of corrupt minds, reprobate concerning the faith. But they shall proceed no further: for their folly shall be manifest unto all men, as theirs also was."* (KJV, 2024).

I want to share a concept with you that we are experiencing in churches everywhere we travel now. My husband and I have been watching as the "Spirit of Jannes and Jambre" tries to operate in every church we have ministered in. We have noticed that many of the pastors were aware of this spirit's influence and were trying to battle against its actions, but did not understand how to bind and stop it successfully.

We have a prayer list with over 300 names on it, where these ministers have requested prayer for their ministries and churches, asking for spiritual support to battle these spirits of opposition. They are aware that this is an attack of Satan, but they are battling so many spirits in the church that they are trying to discredit the pastor and pastoral staff.

> <u>Matthew 7:21-23</u>—"Not everyone that saith unto me, Lord, Lord, shall enter into the kingdom of heaven; but he that doeth the will of my Father which is in heaven. Many will say to me on that day, Lord, have we not prophesied in thy name? And in thy name have cast out devils? And in thy name have done many wonderful works? And then will I profess unto them, I never knew you: depart from me, ye that work iniquity." (KJV, 2024).

I am confident that you know everyone is not going to Heaven. According to this scripture, people will go in the name of Jesus, claiming his miracle power, anointing, and prophecy in Jesus' name, knowing that they have "secret sins" in their lives. I witness weekly ministers standing in their pulpits under the influence of the spirit of "spiritual witchcraft," controlling their members, including their money.

Recently, I watched a pastor's wife take the pulpit one Sunday morning to make announcements and sat there in shock as she went into a "manipulative-spiritual-witchcraft" mode. She told the membership that she wanted to motivate them to give $68 to her husband for his 68th birthday. She then told them that, in addition to their monetary gift, they needed to go to the store, buy whatever they wanted the most, and then give it to her husband. She provided examples: a new tux, a Rolex, a new computer, an iPad, new golf clubs, and a golf cart, among others. Her list was extensive. She informed them that buying what they desired the most and giving it to the man of God was the quickest way to get God's attention on their life and finances.

Most people do not recognize this spirit. However, I began to pray. I had to preach after this demonstration she was giving. I was dreading the spiritual "feet-in-the-mud" attitudes and resistance that I was sure I would feel. I started binding spirits when the Holy Ghost said, "Open your eyes and look around." So, I opened my eyes. When I did, I noticed that six of these six members had been so "brain-washed" by this pastoral team that they did not recognize that they were being played. (I later discovered she raised over $1 million for his birthday!)

No one resisted; they shouted Amen and cheered her on. She continued her performance on the scale of a large pep rally before a high school football game. When she finished, most of the church was on their feet, clapping and chanting, "Happy Birthday, Prophet X."

I had never seen a church so deceived by this controlling spirit. The sermon I prepared to preach at this church addressed why, as a church, we do not see miracles, victories, and souls saved in our churches. As I prepared my sermon, the Lord prompted me to share the story about the "*First Church of God of Babylon*" that Charlie O'Neal (2021) shared in his book, "**The Spiritual Warrior.**" I had shared with my mother and husband on the way to this church that morning that the Lord had told me to read the story from the first chapter of that book. Not to tell the story but to read it. That was something that I had never done before. I have summarized the thoughts of other pastors and authors (giving them credit for their ideas), but I had never read three pages from a book from the pulpit.

Even though I knew God said to do that, I was second-guessing myself. My husband looked at me and said, "Are you sure? How long is the story?" So, I began reading it to him and his mother. When I finished the story, Momma shared a dream she had had the night before. That dream was so similar to this author's story that I took that as a "witness of the spirit" that the story was on the right track.

I remember being so nervous when I started that morning. However, when I began reading the story (reprinted with permission from HFT Publishing, Inc. and Charlie O'Neal at the end of this chapter—make sure to read it; it's an excellent story), I was impressed. The power of the Holy Ghost was felt in that service. When I looked up, the Pastor and his wife were both at the altar before me, asking for prayer. I stopped preaching and began praying over them. The spirit moved, and a word of prophecy was given over the two of them. They repented that day and began working on making changes. It was not an overnight success—Satan's imps did not want to let go of them. I spent many days and evenings on the phone praying with them over the next year, binding spirits and breaking oppressions.

Please remember this scripture: "Not everyone who says to me, Lord, Lord, will enter the kingdom of Heaven," and only those who do the will of the Heavenly Father will enter! Many will appear at Heaven's gates, thinking they will gain entrance, only to discover that their deceptive works and self-centeredness will not be allowed in Heaven's gates.

I know that it sounds like I am a "doom and gloom" preacher. I receive frequent inquiries from people asking why I don't write books like Joel Osteen and David Jeremiah. I love both authors and read every book they publish each year. My favorite author is Max Lucado. I do not miss one of his books—but their calling is not mine! I am not writing to compete with other Christian authors. I am writing to share with the church what God has revealed to me.

You may even question why I have chosen passages from the New Testament for this book. However, I want everyone God allows to cross my path or read my books to understand that in these last days, a lying spirit will deceive devout Christians with false truths to ensure that as many miss the rapture as possible!

The scriptures I have chosen show that we do not have to run in fear of these spirits or Satan's strategies. The Holy Spirit empowers us to take control over these oppressive spirits. We do not have to give in to the devil's intimidation, bullying, or blackmail. These scriptures assure us that we have the power to stop these spirits in their tracks. We have the power to put the Devil on the road! These scriptures show that we are wide open to the attack of this oppressive spirit and its deceptions unless we put on the whole armor of God daily and agree with God's word that we are overcomers through the blood of Jesus Christ!

The influence that opposing spirits have includes the "trickle-down effect." Once a person is deceived, they deceive others without realizing it. The deceived persons tell others the "fake truths" they have learned. Once they are convinced that a "fake truth" is the truth they will argue and debate with others until they convince them of the fake truth. It is incredible how Satan convinces people of his lies. If we do not plant the word of God in our hearts, this deception becomes easy. Paul warned the Corinthians that they could be turned over to a reprobate mind to believe their created lies. Playing with lies and deceitfulness is playing with fire!

In these last days, a pastor, the church's leadership team, and the board need the gift of discernment. It is imperative that we recognize these demonic influencers and stop their operations in our churches. This gift of discernment will enable anyone to identify those operating under a supernatural power other than the Holy Spirit.

In **II Timothy 3:7-9,** the Apostle Paul compares the Old Testament figures Jannes and Jambres to the deceivers and false teachers who would appear in the last days. Paul was trying to get Timothy to understand that sorcery, demonic powers, and other evil spirits could masquerade as a godly spirit. They can take on a form of godliness that makes them appear sheep, but they are wolves in sheep's clothing, deceiving those around them. In other words, these people claim to know and understand the power of God, but they are denying God's power and giving praise to Satan.

Paul warns Timothy of this spirit of opposition and its desire to lead the church into the realm of the demonic, rather than into spiritual victory. If you are honest with yourself, you have already met a few people like this in your Christian Walk. There are many out there going in the name of the church, especially in the Charismatic and Pentecostal circles, where they can use the words "God said, God showed me, God spoke to me, or Thus saith the Lord," phrases that put fear in the hearts of the common man and woman.

People under the influence of the spirit of Jannes and Jambre use Christian words, claims, phrases, examples, and scriptures to "scare" people into complying with their teachings or taking the actions they want them to engage in. For example, consider giving money or planting a seed. Recently, we have been seeing a growing promotion of providing "gifts" to pastors and ministers for all of the special occasions in their lives.

The spirit of Jannes and Jambre deceptively opposes by sharing false truths. In other words, they make Christian claims and use Christian words and phrases, but there is no godly reality in their life. The comparison with Jannes and Jambres certainly brings in the element of demonic involvement.

It is amazing to me how Satan and "False Prophets" like to attract unmarried women who have sorted sexual past into their groups. Typically, these women are gullible and vulnerable to any group that shows them love and acceptance, as most church groups tend to be critical of them. These false teachers will accept all of the questionable characters and highly utilize them. It is amazing how comfortable they can make individuals and how easily they can bond with them.

Once a bond has been established, these false teachers will begin deceiving them. In some churches, they will get these women indebted to them sexually and financially. Once these women are dependent on them, they begin controlling them and abusing them.

Once these individuals are under their control, they begin to teach them how to appear spiritual, use their gifts to gain people's favor, and "endow" those individuals with them. This spirit is drawn to women because of their emotional and compassionate nature. Most women attracted to these spirits are hungry for love and acceptance. This makes it easy for them to be manipulated and used to control certain members, leadership staff, and the church board. (Read Matthew 12 for more insight.)

Deliverance:

Deliverance only comes with Godly sorrow and repentance. Read II Corinthians 7, Acts 2, and Acts 5. Re-read the story of Simon, the sorcerer, if you do not recall how he repented. (II Thessalonians 3).

Remember, the demons in the lives of Jannes and Jambre empowered them to repeat Moses and Aaron's miracles. Its purpose was to keep the children of Israel in bondage and bound to sin, which is what it wants to do to you today. Satan does not want you to live a victorious life. He does not want you to repent or to have hope through Jesus Christ. Satan wants you in bondage, sick, depressed, broke, and suffering. But there is hope through Jesus—repent and ask for Jesus' help to walk away from these spirits. Remember—the rapture is nearer than you think—repent while you still have a chance—tomorrow may be too late!

Repent and ask God to help you lead others back to the cross. Ask God to anoint you to help others open their eyes and see the false teachers and preachers around them.

What Can We Learn from Jannes and Jambres?

What do we learn about these magicians in Exodus? We know that Pharaoh relied on them to oppose Aaron and Moses. They replicated some of the plagues, such as the river of blood, bringing frogs out of the Nile, and turning the dust into gnats. However, they were unable to replicate any of the other plagues. This suggests limits to their powers or that they used "copycat tricks" for the plagues they imitated.

Beyond this, the Bible doesn't say much. We must consider what extrabiblical tradition or ancient history reveals if we seek more details. While these sources don't carry the same weight as Scripture, they can be invaluable when they complement Scripture.

Hopefully, Jannes and Jambres are not the types of Christians you are trying to be. We do not want to be "fake truth" sharers or active spirits opposing God's work. I pray that you recognize the power of this spirit and that you distance yourself from anyone who demonstrates this spirit in their life. They are no match for the real power of God. Unless they repent, destruction is coming. Do not get caught in the fallout. Repent and walk away!

Do not fall for fake imitations of the power of God. Do not accept those cheap "knock-offs" as the genuine power of God. God's power cannot be outdone. Do not be deceived by the "fake power" and spiritual gifts that this spirit displays. Remember, God has the power to bring plagues and deliverance simultaneously!

People can appear to change. They can tell you that they have changed. But do not be deceived. Watch for the fruits of the Spirit in their lives. Be aware and look for the works of the flesh, deception, and lying. People love to "turn over a new leaf" without repenting and changing. They do this to lead people away from the truth and the real anointing.

CHAPTER FOUR:

Can the spirit of Jannes and Jambres affect us?

One of the best ways to learn about spirits and how they operate is to look at the stories of the Bible. Before I discuss the impact that the spirits of Jannes and Jambre will have in the last days, as they support the Spirit of Jezebel, the Spirit of Babylon, and other spirits, I refer you to a book that may help you understand what happened during the Exodus. I am sure that many of you have watched the NBC series written by Roma Downey and Mark Burnett.

This epic TV miniseries, "***The Bible***" (2013), shared many historical and cultural customs of that day. This book is written as a fictional novel. The mini-series followed the book closely. I have watched the series many times. I have the complete series on DVD. However, over a year ago, I found a copy of the hardback book at a Goodwill store and have thoroughly enjoyed reading it. The book contains more details than could be incorporated into the mini-series.

Downey & Burnett (2013) discuss, in detail, part two, "The Exodus," of the Israelites' journey from Egypt to the Holy Land. They delve into history and fill in the gaps from Moses' writing with "possible ways" that this story could have unfolded. We will never know the details until we get to heaven. However, when you look closely at the customs and cultural aspects of life in a country or with an ethnic group, it is easy to imagine how the story went—and pretty accurately, I might add.

Moses had to have been raised with other children in the Palace. I am confident that the current Pharaoh (brother of the Princess who adopted Moses) had children. He would have needed an heir to his throne. There is a possibility that a "sibling rivalry" similar to the one they predicted occurred. If not, at the very least, Ramses would have known Moses. All his weaknesses, flaws, faults, and strengths. This knowledge impacted Moses' presentation before Ramses, the Pharaoh whom Moses and Aaron went before.

It is hard for our families to accept words of knowledge, wisdom, and revelations from God from us today. Imagine those family members knowing your criminal past, insecurities, speech impediments, physical disabilities, etc. Understanding this helps you to realize why Moses questioned God so intently as to why he was the one chosen to lead the children of Israel out of Egypt's bondage.

Understanding this childhood rivalry or competition also helps you to grasp why Pharaoh would have wanted the magicians, wise men, nobles, and sorcerers to double-check behind Moses and Aaron's miracles. I am certain that Ramses was not planning to accept any words from Moses and Aaron without further investigation and scrutiny.

As you read the story created by Downey & Burnett (2013), you will gain a thorough understanding of Moses' debate with God and Ramses' difficulty in listening to Moses and Aaron. Even though this novel does not name Jannes and Jambre, it shares with the reader how Jannes and Jambre recreated the miracles that Aaron performed, including the staff of Aaron consuming the staffs (snakes) of the magicians.

Take a moment to read part two of the book. If you do not have the book or the DVDs, sign in to your Prime Video or Netflix account and search for this mini-series. It will be worth the investment of your time to re-watch this mini-series to help you understand this book and its purpose of teaching you how to recognize the oppressive spirit of Jannes and Jambre.

How will this spirit affect people in the last days?

As you read through the book of Revelation and run references back to II Timothy and II Thessalonians, it becomes evident that there will be a number of false prophets, false teachers, anti-Christs, and others claiming to be Jesus who will come out with power and a toolbox full of tricks and miracles that they can perform to deceive people in the last days.

Revelation talks about the whore of Babylon, Jezebel, and the great deceiver, the beast, Satan. Every mention of someone evil in the book of

Revelation is to warn us that these spirits will be trying to deceive the Christians and keep the non-believers from accepting the fact that Jesus will return to get his children. Satan does not want us to know or understand that in the end, He (Satan) loses, and we (the children of God, redeemed by his son, Jesus Christ) win in the end!

The Book of Revelation is essentially a love letter from Jesus to his church. It warns us of the dangers ahead, prepares us for what we will face, equips us with knowledge of how to overcome, and encourages us to press forward, not giving up, like a runner in a race—staying true to the course, not looking back.

With an incredible love letter, like the book of Revelation, we can be guaranteed our deliverance and victories. This book outlines the final showdown between Jesus and Satan. It covers both weaknesses and strengths. Revelation foretells that Satan's power will increase, and his influence will increase significantly in the last days. Satan will also increase his persecution of the Christians and Jews. However, we must stand fast, unmovable—to the death!

We must understand that we are chosen by God. He has put his hedge of protection around us. We are the only ones who can destroy that hedge. We are the only ones who can allow Satan to control our lives, homes, careers, and ministries. The book of Revelation concludes with the awe-inspiring news of how the battle between Satan and Jesus ultimately ends—we win! If we give our hearts and lives to God, he will spiritually protect us. Even if we give our lives for the gospel's sake, we will gain our heavenly life and rewards. God also promises that when he returns back to earth—the second coming of Christ—all evil will be destroyed, and there will be peace, joy, glory, blessings, and prosperity for 1000 years.

The entire Bible is filled with promises of what God will do for us if we ask for His help. It also shares with us how we can achieve victories in our lives despite the trials we face. I have listed several scriptures that I would like you to study when possible. Read the entire chapter. Read it, then pray over it. Read it a second time. Let God speak to your heart and give you insight into how we can live victoriously without spirits of oppression hindering our journey.

>
> Psalms 91
> Matthew 24:1-14, and 36-44
> Luke 18:8
> Romans 10:13
> I Corinthians 4:5
> I John 2:18

Daniel 12:4
Isaiah 46:10
John 6:39
Hebrew 1:1-2
II Peter 3:3-4
II Timothy 3:1-5
II Timothy 4:1-3
Jude 1:7
Revelation1:1-7
Revelation 13:16-18
Revelation 21:8

Once you have read these scriptures, you will see the promises of God and how we are victorious by the words of our testimony and the intent of our hearts. Do not let anyone or any group of people discourage you.

In the post-COVID world, the evangelical church is suffering. Almost every preacher you hear on TV shares statistics from their organization or one of the popular Christian magazine polls. It is challenging to obtain an accurate set of statistics because not all major players are willing to share their data, fearing that their ministers may become discouraged and abandon their churches.

However, we must stop worrying about our public image and share the good, the bad, and the ugly statistics with our churches. We need to hold strategy meetings, determine what our communities need, and then redesign our church outreach ministries to meet those needs. That means it will be different for each community. There is no way to write a book that will answer the questions of every church and show how to design your church to survive in the post-COVID world.

In the 1990s and early 2000s, every church within an organization attempted to replicate the success of the churches within it. If it worked in Phoenix, AZ, it should work in Mobile, AL. However, that is not how it works. There is no "one-size-fits-all" recipe for mapping out what the pastor needs to do. We have become so business-minded that we have forgotten that our key resource is God. We should be asking God what he wants for our church. Asking God about which of our community's needs he wants us to focus on.

If a pastor, board, and leadership team fail to search for and identify the community's needs, they will fail to ask God to reveal which needs the church should address. We need to reconsider our mission and close our doors if everyone is not willing to follow what God is asking of the church.

We are not a social club where membership provides access to the best local jobs, the right political connections, and bragging rights. We should all be humble servants of God, trying to snatch every lost soul from the hands of Satan every day. We should be the prayer warriors and spiritual warriors who are trying to storm the gates of hell, stand and bind Satan and his imps, and bring deliverance to our members and the community. We should be promoting faith, not fear; love, not doubt; resources, not sucking the membership's finances dry.

Each time I read over these notes, I am reminded of a sermon my father preached years ago. He ended the sermon with a statement and a question. What would be the results if your life went before God's throne for review today? Would God be happy with what you have done, how you are doing it, and what you have accomplished, or would he say, "I am sorry, I do not know you!"

The Houston Herald (2024) stated that "churches are closing rapidly in the US." This article says that the reason for this increasing number of closings is that younger generations are abandoning their families' Christian heritages, while more liberal political views are influencing them. This article outlines how the COVID-19 pandemic accelerated the closing of many of these churches. This article states that many church buildings are now for sale, with the majority going for different purposes.

In our area, I have seen churches converted to indoor flea markets and housing for the homeless. I visited one Baptist church that had since closed. The new buyers converted the building into a halfway house, with each Sunday School room converted to apartments for the residents.

According to the Houston Herald (2024), approximately 4500 Protestant churches closed in 2019. Lifeway Research also claimed that 3000 new church buildings were opened in 2019. Most researchers believe that this trend, which began in 2019, will continue through 2030, as it has since the COVID-19 pandemic. (I am writing this book in 2024. There has been a steady decline in churches and the number of ministers seeking licensure in the organization with which I am licensed this year.)

According to the Houston Herald (2013), Scott McConnell, executive director at Lifeway Research, stated that the COVID-19 pandemic closures, even though temporary, had a lasting impact on churches because of "people breaking their habit of attending church means many churches had to work hard to get people back to attending again."

The Survey Center on American Life and the University of Chicago, in the Spring of 2022 (The Houston Herald updated this article in February 2024 to add these statistics), stated that "Protestant pastors reported that typical church attendance is ONLY 95% of pre-pandemic [attendance] levels, with 67% of Americans reporting attendance at church at least once a year, compared with 75% before the pandemic.

According to the Houston Herald, the 2017 Lifeway survey surveyed young adults (18-22) who attended church regularly for at least a year during high school. They found that seven out of 10 had stopped attending church regularly. There is a definite shift in the church preferences of younger generations. Many are now attending college or living independently and are no longer under the influence of parents who push them to attend church.

ChristianPost.com author Lombardi Blair (2024) reported in his January 11, 2024, article that over half of American pastors have considered leaving the ministry completely. They reported spiritual and physical exhaustion as leading factors. Many complain that the COVID-19 pandemic has made it so complicated that they lack the energy or resources to continue. With this crisis in the pulpits, what can we expect in the pews?

That is correct! Mass exodus! Satan knew when he encouraged churches to close in 2020 that many would never reopen. How would these churches survive with the mass exodus of the last three generations from the weekly church scene? During this pandemic, legends of oppressive demons emerged, similar to the oppressive spirits of Jannes and Jambre, which were released upon America.

These oppressive spirits have been targeting the membership and church leadership teams. These spirits have been released since March 2020 in massive numbers to oppress the church members. Destroy the finances of the churches and the membership, and oppose the truth to a woke agenda that is repressive, making elderly members feel that there is no reason to continue to fight to keep the churches open.

In the area where we live in south Alabama, I have seen eight large evangelical churches and ten rural evangelical churches close since the pandemic ended. Some buildings were sold to other church groups, but they have struggled to succeed. Some church buildings that got a second chance with a different denomination have now closed. In one town, two evangelical church buildings are in a state of disrepair. There is no money to keep the building up while waiting for a sale.

Then, here in Brewton, we watched in shock at the announcement that the Church of God church in Downtown Brewton will close on 12-31-2024, not because of the lack of members or a pastor but because the trust that owns the building is not renewing its lease because it wants the building to have a non-religious focus as a historical building for 2025. What is happening?

This oppressive spirit of Jannes and Jambre is convincing the people of our area of a "fake truth" or "fake future" that we can stand up and declare will not be our future! It will not be our destiny if we stand and bind this opposing and oppressive spirit that wants us to give up and sit down. The post-COVID church has to develop a warrior mentality. We must stand and fight for our churches, our children, our communities, and all our family and friends who have yet to find salvation.

So, yes, the spirit of Jannes and Jambre will have a major impact in the last days—it has already started! This opposing spirit, along with the other major oppressive, retaliating, jealous, and destructive spirits, is joining forces. Unless the church of America rises and says, "***Enough is enough! No more! We are not leaving our pea patch (or churches and communities) again!***" We will see an even more significant mass exodus from our churches if we do not join together and fight. Refer to the story of Gideon in the Old Testament. Gideon was so upset over the Philistines coming in and stealing their crops. God told him to stand and fight. He did—alone at first—then others were motivated and inspired by his stand.

If we fail to develop the "Gideon Warrior Complex," we will continue to see churches close and ministers not renew their licenses, instead walking away from ministry completely. It is time for the church to put on the whole armor of God, get organized, and arm itself for battle! We can take America back from Satan. We can take our families back from the devil.

The Apostle Paul wrote some of the best letters in the New Testament. He was continually trying to encourage the churches and keep them motivated to stay in the fight. It was much harder for them than for us today. Each time they went to church or gathered to read one of Paul's letters, they risked their lives. They knew they could be beheaded for sharing the good news of the gospel of Jesus Christ—but they witnessed it anyway! Are we this determined? Are we this type of spiritual warrior?

We no longer have to sit around and be run over by the "woke community" that says we cannot preach the gospel of Jesus Christ. We no longer have to soft-soak our sermons, fearing that we will lose more members than we did during the pandemic. We must take a stand. We must re-strategize and plan how we will survive in a post-COVID world. We must learn how to reach the younger generation with the church. They are not coming to the church—we must go to them.

We need to know the community's needs, where our churches are located, and how we can help meet those needs. What can the church do to support the community? Pre-COVID, it was what the community could do for the churches and what the members could do for the pastors. That changed! We need to forget about $1,500 suits, $5,000 shoes, luxury cars, Rolex watches, and diamonds. We must return to simplicity and focus on ministry, not images and deities.

The elaborate lifestyles of TV preachers are now a thing of the past! Yes, some are still fighting to maintain their extravagant lifestyles, and they will always be around. Still, in the post-COVID world, we will see fewer Jim and Tammy Bakker couples, fewer Jimmy Swaggart "fighting machines," and more humble ministers with a focus on helping people, salvation, and victorious living—not on things and money. This is the focus God desires for his children.

In 2024, the Assemblies of God published statistics for their organization, which included the 2023 numbers. License renewal is in October of each year. Churches have until mid-January of next year to submit their church stats. So, in the first quarter of 2024, the 2023 stats arrived. It will be interesting to see how much our organization will change between 2025 and 2030. I found it extremely interesting that the Assemblies of God website (https://ag.org/about/statistics) did not cover statistics for pre- or post-COVID periods. It appears that they do not want to discuss those numbers. From national surveys conducted by major pollsters, we know they included all the large Assemblies of God and Church of God churches. Yet, each one avoids reporting stats outside of its organization.

Here are the Assembly of God 2023 stats for US Churches:

2,984,352 members
12,681 churches
37,885 ministers
51% of members are under the age of 35
44% of members are an ethnic minority
5,221 missionaries

Here are the 2023 Assembly of God Worldwide Fellowship Stats:

450,106 churches
436,337 ministers
86,143,293 members

As you can see, the Assemblies of God is greater internationally than in the United States. This organization started in the US and began to spread internationally in the 1960s. It is remarkable to see that they have expanded internationally, with fewer than 10 percent of their ministers residing in the United States. With less than 3 million US members in comparison to the 86 million international members, it is easy to see that the US Assembly of God churches are suffering post-COVID, like all the US Protestant organizations.

I share these statistics not to depress you or to discourage your church attendance. I share them to show you how Satan is working and what his goal is for the church of America: complacency, depression, oppression, discouragement, dwindling membership, and resources, so he can convince them to accept the "woke agenda" so that numbers will increase and revenue return.

Satan's goal is to sell the church of America "*A Fake Truth*" that it is ok to accept the woke agenda and to accept everyone, letting God be the judge, not us. Satan wants us to believe that it is ok to stay away from controversial issues so that we do not offend anyone and let each person work out their standards and convictions by what works best for them.

La Wanda Blackmon

CHAPTER FIVE:

How can we be protected from this spirit?

There are many ways to protect our homes. If you Google the topic, you will find a variety of methods, including crystals, dream catchers, spiritual healers, spirit cleansers, and many other new-age strategies. Do not be deceived. These are not the answers to cleansing your home of evil spirits and breaking ties that these spirits establish with us and our family members.

The best way to get freedom from any spirit is through prayer, fasting, and standing firmly on the word of God. When we quote God's word to Satan, he has to comply. We have power and authority over all types of spirits through the power of the Holy Spirit and the word of God (the Bible).

Spirits easily attach themselves to us when we let down our guard, stop reading and praying, or begin to grumble and complain. Any negative words that exit our mouths open the door for Satan to come into our homes and start oppressing us. The Holy Spirit puts a hedge around us that Satan cannot cross. If we let our guard down, he can compromise our finances, health, children, jobs, homes, possessions, and more.

There is nothing wrong with admitting that you have let the guard down. It does not mean that you are a terrible person. Satan will use pride to keep us from getting help and re-establishing the hedge. Satan loves to convince people that there is no use in believing that things have always been this way and that, without bad luck, we would not have any luck at all.

When Satan or your best friend tells you these words, rebuke them in the Name of Jesus, cancel those words, and speak truth to the situation. Then, pray and bind this spirit and any other spirits that it has brought with it to your home.

At least once per year, my husband and I anoint all our house doors, windows, and appliances. We walk our property line and anoint all the buildings, equipment, vehicles, and other things we possess. We put a hedge around it. We ask God to extend the life of cars and appliances so that they last longer than we could have thought or imagined. We ask for God's blessings on our home, finances, jobs, health, and all that we have. We make sure that we keep this hedge around us.

We are sometimes tried and tested—we are not exempt from trials and tests because of our beliefs or that we claim to be a Christian. God allows us to be tested, as Job was, so that we can appreciate His love, grace, and mercy. We are tested to ensure that God is in first place in our lives. Getting our priorities out of alignment with God's word is easy. When this happens, things begin to go wrong. At any time, we are tested—regardless of the reason—we begin to pray and search our lives. Sometimes, we need to reprioritize and start over. At other times, God witnesses that He is just checking to see that we still love Him more than anything or anyone else in our lives.

God, Jehovah, is a jealous God. He will not tolerate anything or anyone being above him. If things and possessions are hindering you, be prepared; God will remove those possessions or jobs from your life. God wants us to be dedicated to him. This does not mean we cannot be blessed or enjoy life. But we must keep God first.

It is easy to say that you have God first. However, it is harder to prove. It is hard to sacrifice and do without to do something for someone else. It is hard to spend time with God when it would be more fulfilling to go shopping or take a vacation. However, God honors our sacrifices, regardless of their size. The seeds we plant into our heavenly home and retirement are more valuable than those we plant in this life!

II Samuel 23:8-12—These *be* the names of the mighty men whom David had: The Tachmonite that sat in the seat, chief among the captains;

> the same was Adino the Eznite: *he lifts up his spear* against eight hundred, whom he slew at one time. And after him was Eleazar the son of Dodo the Ahohite, *one* of the three mighty men with David, when they defied the Philistines *that* were there gathered together to battle, and the men of Israel were gone away: He arose, and smote the Philistines until his hand was weary, and his hand clave unto the sword: and the LORD wrought a great victory that day; and the people returned after him only to spoil. And after him was Shammah, the son of Agee the Hararite. And the Philistines were gathered together into a troop, where was a piece of ground full of lentiles: and the people fled from the Philistines. But he stood in the midst of the ground, and defended it, and slew the Philistines: and the LORD wrought a great victory. (KJV, 2024).

The father of King David was Jesse. Jesse had seven sons. David's six brothers were:

Eliab, the oldest
Abinadab
Shimea (Shammah)
Nethanel
Raddai
Ozem
David was the seventh son

The prophet Samuel anointed David, the youngest of Jesse's sons (a ruddy young boy), who tended the sheep for his father. Many years later, when it was time for David to become King of Israel, King Saul was unwilling to give up the throne. He fought to his dying breath to keep his throne. During these years, as God was grooming and training David, Saul was trying to kill him. David went into the wilderness as he ran for his life from King Saul. God dealt with and drew men to David. Most were men in trouble, financial ruin, or running from someone or something. Today, we would call them a renegade bunch of mercenaries.

However, David was a man of faith. He did not understand the words "it's too hard" or the words "I cannot do that!" David took these renegades and began training them. David taught them to be giant, lion, and bear killers! David trained them in covert operations. He trained them to fight under the anointing of God, consecrated to God while being wise as a serpent!

David taught his men not to be afraid! The book of II Samuel lists 37 mighty men of honorable mention whom David had trained. It lists the top three, then thirty mighty men. Please pay close attention to how the verses of II Samuel list these men and their qualifications.

Of this list of men, I want you to pay close attention to the number three man—Shammah. This is not the Shemia or Shammah who was David's brother. This was Shammah, the son of Agee, the Hararite. He was David's number three among his mighty men. To be number three and appreciate that position out of thirty-seven, you need to understand the qualifications of the first two men.

The number one guy was Adino, the Eznite. This guy was so mighty that he fought 800 men by himself at one time. He killed all 800 men! Can you imagine? I cannot even imagine how much energy it took to kill 800 men without stopping or taking a break. We think it is horrible if three people gang up on one person. I cannot even imagine 800 men!

Eleazar, the son of Dodo, the Ahohite, was the second-in-command. The scripture says that he was such a fighter that he fought until the last Philistine in the army that day was dead or gone. He fought for so long that his hand was "frozen" to the sword. He could not even remove his hand. The scripture says there was a great victory that day in Israel, and when he finished fighting, the people returned to spoil the land of the Philistines.

> *Shammah, the son of Agee, the Hararite, was one of David's mighty men. After he came to David in the wilderness for training, David trained them to be giant killers. These men would kill large numbers of men at a time. David had trained them to be mighty warriors capable of killing Giants, lions, and bears. We have been called to be mighty warriors—spiritual warriors for the Kingdom of Heaven.*

> *God is waiting for us to say that we have left our "pea patch" (field of lentils) for the last time! Then the anointing comes. Where is your faith? Where is your warrior spirit? The Holy Ghost has come through Jesus Christ!*

    I have heard my father preach on this scripture several times during the 1960s and 1970s. As I conducted research for this book, I searched online to find other preachers with sermons available online that I could recommend on this topic. Of the ten I saw, I chose one for you.

    I found a Camp Meeting Service from Jimmy Swaggart Ministries in Baton Rouge, LA on *YouTube*. I have no idea when this sermon was preached. Judging by the hairstyles and clothes of the audience, I think this was the late 1990s or early 2000s camp meeting service. The reference for this video is "***Jimmy Swaggart: I've left this pea patch for the last time.***" It was posted to YouTube on March 20, 2011.

    Jimmy Swaggart preaches for about 55 minutes in this video. He rambles on several topics during the sermon, but makes some excellent points. These are some of the same points that I recall my father preaching in years past. He also shares some of the same genealogy components I shared above with you. Make sure that you listen to the entire program. He begins with some of the facts I have provided, then shares stories and testimonies that will encourage you. He closes this sermon strongly, enabling us to stand our ground spiritually and not leave our pea patch or inheritance.

    This YouTube video does not get into the spiritual warfare concepts that I have covered. However, other references and books are available on Amazon, which I mentioned in a previous chapter, and you can refer to them. The more research you do—the more you learn—the greater warrior you will be in these last days. The greater chance you have of helping your children and family avoid the snares set by Satan to keep us from being "rapture-ready!" I highly recommend the spiritual warfare books by Charlie O'Neal and Jennifer LeClaire, which are listed for sale on Amazon. Kindle versions are also available.

    However, there are a couple of facts that I want you to remember from this scripture text and this sermon. **The first fact** is that fear kills faith, rendering it completely useless and powerless. Faith requires perfect love for our heavenly Father. David taught his warriors this concept. It was God, first and foremost, with them all the time. As a result, they were anointed with a powerful anointing and hedge of protection around David and his men the entire time they were on the run from King Saul.

The second fact is that we must be resolute in our determination not to walk away from our heritage, inheritance, or God's will for our lives, regardless of who they might be, no matter how powerful they may be. David's men knew that they were devoted to David, irrespective of what King Saul did or said. Nothing was changing that! That is the mindset of Shammah when he said he was not leaving his pea patch (lentil patch) anymore and letting the enemy have his harvest.

Until we can develop a "warrior mentality," we do not entirely grasp what I am saying here. Determination, stickability, dependability, loyalty, and commitment are just a few words that come to mind when Shammah's name is mentioned.

How to protect from and break the power of the spirit of Jannes and Jambre:

Everyone wants to know how to defend their homes and families. Everybody begins to quiver as fear grips them when I begin talking about spiritual warfare. There is nothing to fear. Fear is of Satan. It is his number one tool for preventing us from achieving victory. If we are frozen in fear, we cannot speak the word of God, we cannot pray, and we definitely cannot use our spiritual shield and sword to ward off the darts/arrows that Satan is throwing against our minds and hearts.

Whenever I feel the need to break the evil supernatural powers that are affecting our lives, homes, jobs, families, and so on, I begin praying. I ask the Holy Spirit to identify the type of spirit. If you want your prayer to be effective, you have to call Satan out on what he is doing—name the spirit attacking you! Once I know which spirit is attacking me, I begin searching the scriptures to find God's promises regarding deliverance from that particular spirit.

Then, I began studying that spirit. Even if it is a spirit that I have rebuked numerous times. I refresh my knowledge of that spirit in case there is something that I have forgotten. We have to be aware of how Satan works. We need to be mindful of all the tools he uses against us. This helps us to prevent "re-attachment" or future oppression by that spirit.

Sometimes, while re-studying the spirit attacking us, I realize an area where we have let the hedge get a gap. Sometimes, we get so busy that we forget about one of Satan's tricks. Satan loves it when that happens. Satan loves to use family members to trick us into letting our guard down. When this happens, he gets to come in unhindered. Do not let people make you feel ashamed to talk about spirits and how they operate. Some church members will not even discuss spiritual warfare because they are afraid that it will consume their lives. Guess what—that person is already so oppressed by spirits that they have accepted 100% Satan's most incredible "fake truth"—there is nothing to all this spiritual warfare hype!

Spiritual warfare is real and powerful! If it were not powerful, Satan would not be trying to discredit it all the time. Satan does not want us to know how to live victoriously. I will be the first to admit that I am not a specialist in spiritual warfare or a scholar in this field. However, I have experienced the power of spiritual warfare, and I am a devout believer who recognizes the need for the Holy Spirit's daily guidance in this area of my life.

Paul tells us in Ephesians to "put on the whole armor of God—daily!" We are to prepare ourselves and storm the gates of Hell. Does that sound like something that is not important? Does that sound like something that we should do occasionally? No, we are to put on the whole armor of God daily so that we can withstand what Satan sends our way. So that we can be faithful and victorious, walking in truth!

However, this word—spiritual warfare—is the most fought topic of the evangelical church. People do not want to hear about sin, demons, devils, oppression, possession, deliverances, specific prayers, the armor of God, standing on God's word, and scheduled prayer times with God. People, including ministers, frequently tell me it is too much work. God does not require all of that from us. That is why he went to the cross; he fought that battle for us once and for all times, past, present, and future.

That argument of "fake truth" sounds convincing. I wish it were true. It would make things easier. However, that is what Satan wants from us—complacency! Laziness and complacency open the doors of your life and home wide open for Satan and all of his imps to come in and take up residence.

References for spiritual warfare:

Refer to the books listed in my reference section. Some of those books were quoted in this manuscript. Others are just books that I use as a reference to check my work. Although I did not quote them in this book, I have listed the information about them in the reference list so that you can see the books on this topic that I have read and my own research on the subject. You may decide that you want to read some of those books, too.

I find that writing my manuscript, covering the topics God has witnessed to me, helps me. Sometimes, it is all God wants—a book. Other times, it is a sermon—not a book. Reading and studying God's word always calms me and helps me to relax in the spirit. The word of God has that calming effect on us. That is another reason why Satan tries so hard to block us from reading the word of God.

I write from my heart, then I double-check my writing with my research. Once completed, I send the manuscript to my editor. While waiting for her to give me feedback, I went to Amazon and ordered every book I could find using the keywords I had assigned to my manuscript. I love to read behind other authors as much as I love to write.

Sometimes I will buy a book, then throw it away after starting it because the author is not a Christian or is so theologically incorrect that I do not want to complete the book. There are times when I will complete a book because it is so wrong that I feel compelled to warn people about the false theology or prophecy it contains. I have also found several authors on Amazon with good thoughts, and their theology is on track; however, the grammar and organization of their self-published books are so poor that I will not recommend them.

I have found a few books written by some famous elderly ministers on Amazon that were so confusing, I would not recommend them, even though I have read them thoroughly. I respect those ministers and use their words to self-check my writings. I find that reading behind other authors and listening to other ministers helps me. The more "good things" I can put into my brain, the better off I am. It does not matter that I have heard it before. Sometimes, I think I have preached that topic better than the person I am listening to, but it does not matter; I listened anyway. I feel that there is ALWAYS something that I can learn from everyone.

I do not recommend this level of research verification or reading to new converts or individuals new to spiritual warfare. There are too many authors and preachers out there who are confused, some of whom are even false prophets and teachers. That is why I include additional resources in my reference list or mention books in my manuscript that I think would be beneficial for you to read.

However, if you are a seasoned pastor with years of experience or an author, know that prolific research and reading of other authors will continually improve your delivery of this message of hope. We are not in a competition with each other. We are working for the same King, delivering the same message. The more we write, the more we speak, the better we get. The more we research, the more we learn. I firmly believe we should never stop researching and learning, but rather continue until we pass away. You are never too old to learn!

Things to avoid so the spirit of Jannes and Jambre cannot attach to you:

1) Witchcraft
2) Occult activities
3) Occult movies
4) Books on the occult or practice of witchcraft
5) Harry Potter books
6) Ouija boards
7) Native American Indian dream catchers
8) Voodoo dolls
9) Fortune tellers
10) Horoscopes
11) Psychic Hotlines

Let me clarify a couple of things for you. Oppression is different from possession. Demons cannot possess a true man or woman of God who is spirit-filled. They can be demonized and oppressed. The only way they can become possessed is if they let down the hedge that God has placed around them. We can destroy the hedge of protection that God has placed around us through the Holy Spirit by allowing the following things to come into our lives, or by allowing individuals who are controlled by these spirits and demons to take control of our lives.

1) Demonic movies
2) Vampire movies
3) Harry Potter movies or books
4) Horoscopes and/or fortune-telling events
5) Séance
6) Ouija boards, tarot cards
7) Evil movies with violent murders, horror movies,
8) Occult activities, events,
9) Voodoo dolls, occult paraphernalia

Signs and Symptoms of Demonic Oppression:

Oppression is an attack from the outside (outside your life, home, body, church, and family) against you personally, spiritually, emotionally, physically, and financially.

Demonic oppression usually begins as an attack on a person's mind, causing them to worry or stress over situations or circumstances. Demonic oppression usually results in fear and doubt overwhelming the person and causing a "heavy feeling" that feels like it will press the life out of a person.

1) Mental problems and depression
2) Irrational fear
3) Constant anxiety
4) Unexplainable health problems
5) Lack of rest and nightmares
6) Overwhelmed feelings, with extreme exhaustion
7) Untreatable depression that does not respond to clinical meds and counseling

How do these spirits gain access to our minds? How can we keep them out? First, an evil spirit must find an entry point into your mind or home. Most often, these entry points come through things we hear and see, such as movies, TV, negative news broadcasts, and interactions with people who have a negative outlook. We can open our minds to these evil spirits by reading and absorbing demonic information into our minds by reading books or watching movies that involve the occult and occult practices.

Signs and Symptoms of Demonization:

1) Unexplained catastrophic events
2) Unexplained and undiagnosable health conditions
3) Rare diseases without cures
4) Unexplainable financial problems
5) Attitude and mood changes
6) Inability to handle stress or current conditions
7) Inability to concentrate or read God's word
8) Difficulty praying or inability to pray at all
9) Unable to bind spirits
10) Nightmares, night terrors, restlessness, insomnia, and extreme exhaustion

Signs and Symptoms of Demonic Possession:

The first and most important sign of demonic possession is the person's anger and response to you when you tell them that you think they could be demonized or possessed. The possessed person will become violently angry with you and may even ask you to leave their home. If they were true non-possessed, spirit-filled Christians, their response would be something like this—"Oh, no, what have I done that would make you think I am possessed? Is there something in my life that has pulled me away from that intimate place with God? More than anything in my life, I must be rapture-ready. I cannot miss the rapture or heaven. What do I need to do? What needs to change? What has God shown or witnessed to you?"

A true Christian, regardless of their possession or lack thereof, always seeks ways to improve their relationship with God. True Christians always seek ways to draw closer to Jesus daily, rather than fighting and arguing about whether they are ready. Anytime I see a disgruntled, angry Christian, I know they are spewing out false truths, trying to control everyone, or secure the chief positions for themselves. These individuals are not concerned with what the Holy Spirit wants or what is best for the church.

There are other signs of demon possession. The most prominent one is anger, followed by self-centeredness and self-pity. Everything is about them—they do not care about anyone else's problems. Even if you try to tell them about someone's prayer request or need for healing, they will interrupt you to tell you about their problems and how great their needs are—know are already possessed—deceived beyond measure and, in most cases, turned over to a reprobate mind—a mind that willingly accepts the *"fake truths"* Satan has sent to them. It is always about their needs—total self-centeredness.

God does not accept selfishness. The first and most important of the Ten Commandments is to love the Lord our God and only him. There is no room for self-centeredness in heaven. There is no time for taking care of ourselves—we should be busy trying to be ready to go to heaven and seek to know what else we can do for God and those around us, and how to win every soul possible so that no one is lost.

Steps to Deliverance from Oppression:

The first step is to recognize that oppression is Satanic. Recognize that you are being attacked—do not discredit it, but accept it.

The second step is to study the spirit and search the scriptures for what you need to do or stop doing to break this tie.

<u>The third step</u>: Locate the scriptures that you need to quote to Satan that will give you the power and authority to break the oppressive ties of the spirits attached to you or attacking you.

<u>The fourth step</u>: Sit down and write out a prayer that will take authority over the spirit, break its hold on you, and set you free from it. Read this prayer with a sincere heart daily, breaking these spirits' hold on you until you are delivered.

<u>The fifth step</u>: This step is not always necessary. However, we are sometimes attacked by such powerful evil spirits that we need reinforcements to break them. The scripture says that one can put a thousand spirits to flight and that two people can put ten thousand spirits to flight. That lets you realize the power of two or more people agreeing on a particular matter or deliverance.

If you are praying and binding and nothing appears to be happening, you may need reinforcements. Get someone to help you pray, bind, and break the hold of these spirits in your home and life. Please make sure the person joining you is not bound by spirits themselves.

I strongly recommend that the person who joins you is filled with the Holy Ghost with the evidence of speaking in tongues. Some spirits will not respond to anyone who does not have the gifts of the Spirit operating in their lives. We refer to these as "dominant" or "extremely powerful" spirits.

Here are two more scriptures that you can read and study to help you recognize the signs of oppression and these spirits that Satan likes to introduce into our lives.

Luke 13:10-17
I Corinthians 14:33).

Other signs that will help you recognize that an oppressive spirit is attacking you or your family include. At this phase of the attack, it is not attached to you or possessing you, but it is wearing you down so it can control you.

1) Chronic illnesses
2) Mental oppression and mental illnesses
3) Depression, confusion, doubt
4) Inability to reason, and uncontrollable crying
5) Loss of appetite, torment with fear
6) Nightmares, night terrors
7) Restlessness, insomnia

In conclusion, I would like to emphasize a few key points. I want you to remember these key steps. Please do not skip over them, and do not let people convince you they are unnecessary.

You must eliminate the sources of these spirits, replace the spiritual hedge, and block all spirits' entry points. For example, remove pornography, evil movies, and books from your home. Remove tarot cards, Ouija boards, horoscopes, occult books, and movies from your home. Confess any sins known and unknown.

Then pray your cleansing prayer daily. Bind the spirits and render them incapable of operating in your life and home. Once you begin praising and worshiping God (the most crucial step after praying your cleansing prayer), you will find that Satan cannot stand praise and worship. He will have to leave your presence. Satan does not want you reading and praying either. He wants to separate you from God. So, anything you can do to improve your relationship with Jesus puts Satan on the road!

Finally, separate yourself from individuals who make you feel down or depressed after talking with them. Separate yourself from negative individuals. Mark off family and friends from your inner circle who have spirits controlling them and their lives. If they enter your home with spirits attached to them, some of those spirits will stay, trying to get you in the same condition.

Remember that the Bible assures us that those troubled by evil spirits can be and were cured. **Read Luke 6:17-18, 10:19, John 3:8, and Acts 10:38, then thoroughly study them. Then quote Luke 10:19** to Satan. God has given you power and authority over all of the principalities of darkness. Nothing evil shall harm you or control you!

Acts 10:38 tells us that the reason God gave his only son to take our place on the cross at Calvary was so that Satan would be defeated and that we could have the power and authority to withstand Satan and all of his works. Also, remember the following key facts.

Demonic Oppression loves to operate through fear.

Peter told us in **I Peter 5:8** that we need to strive to be alert and keep a sober mind, rooted in the word of God, with praise and worship in our hearts, so that when Satan goes around "like a roaring lion looking for someone to devour" (KJV, 2024), that we will not be his main target. Keeping our mind on the good things of God, helps block the negative words and "fake truths" that Satan loves to plant into our lives.

Satan's favorite place or realm to operate from is from the realm of fear. Intimidation is his second favorite realm. Whenever we allow fear to overtake us and begin to speak, letting fear speak through us, we tear open a hole in our spiritual hedge and armor. Satan and his imps come rushing in. Fear is gasoline to their fire!

When fear is in control, we lose rest and become fatigued. With fatigue, we become vulnerable and unable to quote the scriptures to Satan. As a result, nightmares, PTSD, and night terrors take over. Then depression sets in. Depression is one of Satan's greatest tools in spiritual warfare. He uses it to paralyze us and keep us from completing the task at hand or being in compliance with what God is asking of us or our ministry.

Remember the whole armor of God, as discussed in **Ephesians 6,** and God's promise to us in **I John 4:4.** There is no need to allow fear to paralyze us, dread, and evil to replace our peace and happiness, taking away our blessings and joy. The spirit of oppression, the spirit of opposition, and jealousy work to destroy our love, freedom, and victory through Jesus Christ. This results in our grumbling, complaining, and acting out, destroying God's blessing for us. As spiritual warriors, we must learn to stand against Satan and advocate for justice and righteousness. The Holy Spirit will transform our lives in a way that will cause people to marvel at what God has done, and Satan will flee from us.

However, we must first recognize these spirits at work in our lives. So many cannot discern the presence of opposition, oppression, evil, fear, or "fake truths." Without spiritual discernment, you will never be victorious. So, in the face of opposition from Satan, it is essential to remember that when the spirit of oppression is at work, Christians must discern its presence and take action. The Holy Spirit equips us with discernment, courage, and wisdom to confront and overcome this spirit.

It is crucial to remember that our battle is not against flesh and blood, but against spiritual forces of evil from the realms of darkness. Only God can fight this battle for us, so let us praise and worship him and stand on his word as we break these chains! The Holy Spirit equips us with the armor and authority of God to resist and overcome!

In **Ephesians 6:12**, the apostle Paul reminds us that our struggle is not against flesh and blood, but against the spiritual forces of evil in the heavenly realms. The disciple James tells us in **James 4:7**, that all we have to do is "Submit ourselves to God. Resist the devil, and he will flee from you." If we draw near to God and stand firm without fear, we can resist Satan, and he will have to leave us alone. We can be victorious through Jesus.

The disciple Peter tells us in **I Peter 5:8-9** that as believers, we do not have to be prey to the "roaring lion" of Satan. However, we can remain safe and secure in our faith in God, knowing that His grace is sufficient to strengthen us and help us resist the devil and overcome.

The Apostle Paul tells us in **Romans 8:37-39** that nothing can separate us from the love of God; not demons, evil spirits, man, or any other power on earth can separate us from God if we love and worship him. Paul promises us that we can have God's love, forgiveness, grace, mercy, and protection from all evil attacks. We must love God with all of our heart and soul!

> *"Faith is the victory that overcomes the world...without faith it is impossible to please God...faith is daring your soul to see further than your natural eye can see...[challenging] your mind to believe what is impossible to understand in the natural."* (Hagee, 2023, p. 51).
>
> **Matt Hagee**
> *Spiritual Warfare: Unlock the Supernatural and Access the Promises of God*

Faith is the key that unlocks the doors of Heaven.

Faith destroys fear.

Fear destroys faith.

Follow Paul and Silas' example—when in prison in stocks and bonds—sing!

CHAPTER SIX:

A Spiritual Warfare Prayer

For spiritual warfare to work in your life, you must have faith in God. Faith has been mentioned in several chapters, but bears mentioning again here. We must have faith in the blood of Jesus and faith that the Holy Spirit is always with us. Without faith, you can pray every spiritual warfare prayer published, and none will be effective. You must have faith in your God, Lord, and Savior! You are the only one who can put Satan on the road. You are the only one who can control the input into your brain.

Before you can pray and engage in effective spiritual warfare prayer, you must kneel and pray, asking for forgiveness of any past or present sins that are not under the blood. If you pray a spiritual warfare prayer with unconfessed sins in your life, you open the door for demon possession, not deliverance. I am not saying this to scare you, but to prepare you. None of us wants to live defeated lives. We want to be victorious. So, repent, then read the scriptures that support what you are about to pray over. Then read your prayer.

This may sound like I am too strict or overbearing on this topic. Just know one fact: Satan knows whether your heart is right and if your sins are covered by the blood or not. Satan IS NOT going to respond when you tell him to leave. He will not walk away if the "smell" of sin is on you.

Unconfessed sin renders the blood of Jesus Christ ineffective, and Satan knows that without that blood, he does not have to respond or obey. So, confess your sins and renew your faith by reading the supportive scriptures. With your faith revived, your prayer will be effective.

Doubt and fear work hand in hand to keep us from achieving our goals. I have worked with many people who did not have unconfessed sins in their lives, but their spiritual warfare was not working. So, I would sit down and talk with them. If we are not victorious spiritually, there is a reason. If your car will not crank, there is usually a reason—no gas, a dead battery, an alternator that is not working, etc. The same concept applies to us spiritually. If our faith is dead, our spiritual battery is dead. When we try to crank the car (pray with power), it does not work! I want you to try these three steps (Confess your sins, quote the scripture, then pray). The spiritual warfare prayer I recommend for individuals just beginning to develop their spiritual warrior skills is discussed below, along with the prayer itself.

Once you feel comfortable with this new knowledge, I recommend writing your own personalized prayer for spiritual warfare. List what you are dealing with and the outcome you expect. I sometimes include scriptures in my prayers. Satan hates it when we quote the word of God to him.

After you have completed these three steps and you are still having problems with effective spiritual warfare praying, do not stop or give up. Continue reading this book. When you reach the conclusion, I share a quote from my book **"Broken: Braced for Favor"** (2022) on faith. I remember the day that God gave this to me. I was so excited that I was dancing in my kitchen. I was trying to cook supper and could not wait for my husband to come home.

When Tommy entered the door, I said, "Sit down, get comfortable. I have something to read to you that God gave me. Remember how I told you something was not 'complete' about that manuscript? I have discussed it with the editor several times. I keep moving the publication date. It should have been printed last year, but something was missing. I was praying this morning, and the Lord showed me something I had not done. He said I was disobedient. Well, that was a strong word. I argued with him that I could not tell the pastor that message. I thought it needed to come from the board or one of the associate pastors." My husband responded, 'Yes…' He was aware of my struggle with this word from the Lord.

"Well," I continued, "I told the Lord that if it was him talking to me and not my mind thinking this, to give me a sign (kind of like what Gideon did when he fleeced God in the Old Testament). I told God I needed to know what was missing from that manuscript. I had writer's block on that manuscript. I kept putting it off, having published numerous other books, but I could not figure out what was wrong with that one. God immediately said, "Faith is what is missing—you cannot go from 'Broken' to 'Braced' in my favor without having perfect faith in me. You have shared everything else but faith. Go and sit at your desk, and I will give you the words."

The words began to flow as soon as I picked up the notebook. I was writing so fast, I do not know if I can even read them, but you must listen!" So, Tommy, I went and sat down. I began to read to him what God had given me—another chapter that needed to be added. Well, in the conclusion of this book, I am going to share with you that "faith quote" that God gave me that changed my outlook and life!

Faith is the key! We have to use faith to dance in the face of the devil when he appears to have the upper hand. We can be victorious if we can revive our faith and put on our dancing shoes. When Satan hears us sing praises to God and dance in the spirit because we are full of faith, the battle is no longer fun for him.

Satan wants to dance on the ashes of what was left of our job, our career, our home, our marriage, or our children. Satan saved one servant from each tragedy to carry the message back to Job. Satan was dancing on the ashes of what "had been" in Job's face. But when Job rose up, he borrowed a lamb and cattle to offer a sacrifice to God. (He had to borrow them—all of his were destroyed.) That took faith. I believe that Job made the sacrifice and was able to praise God for all He had done for him, and as a result, Job became happy. What happens when we get happy? We dance! As the song says, we start drinking from our saucer because our cup is overflowing.

As the aroma of the sacrifice went up to heaven with Job's praise, Job got happy. The windows of Heaven opened as he danced around that altar, praising God. Satan began to fume. I can see the smoke blowing out of his eyes and ears! God reduced Satan, not Job, to ashes. So, Job danced around the altar on the ashes of what the devil had built—fear and doubt.

You and I can dance on the ashes of what Satan built in our lives. We can dance on the grave of what was trying to destroy us. But this only occurs with faith. Faith only comes with a relationship with God. So, keep reading!

Please note that the prayer that follows was one I found on a website while searching for information on spiritual warfare. It is a short prayer that covers the basics. This is a great prayer to start with so that you can be delivered from the oppressive spirit of Jannes and Jambre in your life.

I obtained this prayer from the following website:
www.dailyeffectiveprayer.org/spirit-ofoppression/#:~:text=What%20 doesthe%20spirit%20of%20p[[ressopm/HTML

Jennifer LeClaire has written numerous books on spiritual warfare. She has written books filled with prayers and decrees that you can use to pray for specific topics. I will not list those books or prayers here. In this book, I primarily address the spirit of opposition, oppression, and false teachers. There are over 130 different spirits that can attach themselves to a believer. I do not want to overwhelm you as you begin this journey to understand more of what we are facing in these last days. However, I do want you to experience victorious living.

Please refer to the reference list for the books I have found to be the most recommended for individuals when counseling on this topic. I have quoted these books in this one. However, read the books in the reference list to pursue more concepts and ideas. I always recommend that my readers explore other options and references on the same subject. It helps you to learn from all perspectives. However, if you are new to the Christian faith, be cautious about who you listen to (on TV and Radio) and which authors' books you read until you have learned the Bible and its basic concepts and precepts.

Here is the prayer from this website. Note that we have corrected numerous typos and grammatical errors when transferring this prayer into this book. The grammar was so poor that we felt compelled to make changes, so our readers would not feel insulted as they read and used this prayer. Otherwise, the prayer is exactly as provided on this website.

Deliverance prayer for the spiritually oppressed

Almighty God,

I humbly approach Your Throne, burdened by the weight of the spirit of oppression that looms over me. I look to You for deliverance, knowing that only You can set me free. I stand before You, desperate for Your mercy and grace to wash over me.

I acknowledge that I am weak and unable to fight this battle alone, but thanks be to You because You are with me, and I am not alone. The enemy seeks to steal, kill, and destroy, but I know you are greater. I submit myself to Your authority and invite Your Holy Spirit to come and bring deliverance into my life.

In the name of Jesus, I renounce any foothold the enemy has gained in my life. I declare that I am a child of God and have been redeemed by the blood of the Lamb. I break every chain and stronghold placed upon me and command them to be shattered by the power of Your Spirit, in Jesus' Name.

Father, I ask that You would fill me with Your presence and surround me with Your angels to protect me from the schemes of the evil one. I plead the blood of Jesus over every area of my life, covering myself from the top of my head to the soles of my feet.

I declare Your promises over my life, for You have said You will never leave nor forsake me. You are my refuge and strength, a very present help in times of trouble. I trust in You and know that You are fighting on my behalf.

As I bow before Your Throne, I surrender all my fears, worries, and anxieties. I cast them upon You, for You care for me. Thank you for replacing oppression with your peace and filling me with joy that surpasses all understanding.

Thank you for hearing my prayer; the deliverance is already on its way. I choose to trust in Your goodness and wait upon Your perfect timing. In the mighty Name of Jesus, I pray.

Amen.

BOOKS I RECOMMEND TO HELP YOU ON THIS JOURNEY

Johnson, J. (2019). *The power of consecration: A prophetic word to the church.* Shippensburg, PA: Destiny Image.

In this pre-COVID book by Jeremiah Johnson, you will notice a prophetic word similar to the prophetic word by Charlie O'Neal (2019), **"*A Word from God for the Church*."** This prophetic word encourages the reader to spend time with God. To learn the traps of legalism and religion and how the devil uses these tools to deceive the church.

Johnson covers how Satan wants the end-time church to be the "harlot bride," not the "warrior bride." As you read this book, if you are hungry for a move of God in your life and ministry, you will be motivated to give yourselves completely to God and consecrate yourself at a level you have never completed before.

Once you consecrate yourself as a "***Warrior Bride***," your ministry, life, home, career, and finances will change drastically. The opposition that is attacking you will melt away. Deliverance will be yours. But you must desire to be consecrated to God. This book is not for Christians who want to get by, but for those who want to be Victorious.

Even though this was a pre-COVID book, it is more relevant in the post-COVID world of complacency and 'woke culture' than the author realized when writing this book. Get a copy from Amazon and add this to your spiritual warfare library!

Johnson, J. (2023). *The Warrior Bride.* Shippensburg, PA: Destiny Image

Jeremiah Johnson shows the reader how to conquer the five demonic spirits that war against the church in these last days. He covers the duties of the warrior bride and the common hindrances to victorious living. In this dynamic but straightforward book, Jeremiah Johnson lays out a no-nonsense path to deliverance and how to overthrow Satan's attack in your church without being a casualty of war.

Stone, P. (2011). *Purging your house, pruning your family tree: How to rid your home and family of demonic influence and generational oppressions.* Lake Mary, FL: Charisma House.

Perry Stone explains how to rid your home and your inner circle of people of those under the influence of demonic and generational curses. He explains how easy it is to allow things to come into our homes and bring spirits with them. Then he shares the steps for purging your home and taking control back of your life and home as a spiritual warrior with the help of the Holy Spirit. It is a lot to read, but it is worth it if you are unfamiliar with spiritual warfare.

OakRidgeBibleChapel.org. (2021). *Jezebel or Jesus? The church at Thyatira* [July 21, 2021 Online Sermon by Lew Worrad]. Retrieved from https://oakridgebiblechapel.org/jezebel-or-jesus (Retrieved on 4-20-2023).

This article is available online, where you can download and read it for free. You will not have to buy the book or magazine. It is a sermon outline that covers the topic of Jezebel and how this spirit will impact the church in the last days, linking it to other evil spirits that will be released in the preceding days before the rapture, such as the spirit of Jannes and Jambres.

O'Neal, C. (2019). *A word from God for the church.* Brewton, AL: HFT Publishing

    This is a dynamic book that explores a vast array of demonic spirits that have infiltrated the church. This pre-COVID book is essential for the spiritual warriors' POST-COVID library. Evil began to be unleashed in 2008 and has continued at an alarming rate, as it has forced the "woke agenda" on the churches and has tried to destroy Generation Z and the millennial generations' faith in God. This is a must-read!

O'Neal, C. (2020). *"Why am I not living a victorious life?"* Brewton, AL: HFT Publishing

    Charlie O'Neal answers all the questions you have ever asked about your spiritual life and why you cannot have victory. This is a powerful book that can be challenging for some readers to comprehend. O'Neal is firm on controlling your inner circle and who you listen to—family, friends, and preachers. It is his opinion that what we feed our minds influences us and blocks our spiritual, health, and financial blessings.

    I agree with his theology. I have family that does not, because it means that you have to accept the fact that demons are controlling most evangelical churches. This was my second book by him to read. I do not recommend reading this book without reading the "**Word from God for the Church**" first.

O'Neal, C. (2021). *"The Spiritual Warrior."* Brewton, AL: HFT Publishing

    This is the third book I have read by this author. You definitely need to read these three books in order. Without reading them in order, some of the information may appear incomplete. These three books are part of a series on victorious living. They build upon the concepts introduced in the previous book. Great read! It will take you from the Warrior Bride to the Spiritual Warrior Leader for these last days!

CHAPTER SEVEN:

Book Conclusion

As we approach the last days that the church will have on earth, it is becoming increasingly evident that the spirit of deception is at work in the Christian community. Satan knows that his days are numbered and are coming close to an end. He is determined to deceive as many people as possible before Christ puts him in the pit for 1000 years. How Satan is accomplishing this is through "Spiritual Warfare."

Satan is using every tool in his "toolbox" that can be used against Christians. Satan has many (thousands) of tools that he can use. But I call the ones he uses the most "Satan's Seven Seductions" (SSS).

1) Anger/Revenge
2) Deceitfulness
3) Doubt/Fear
4) Envy/Greed
5) Selfishness/Self-Pity
6) Jealousy/Covetousness
7) Spiritual Witchcraft/Evil Spirits

The Apostle Paul said in ***Ephesians 6*** that we needed to put on the whole armor of God each day. He said that we need to put on the following daily:

> <u>Ephesians 6:10-18</u>—Finally, my brethren, be strong in the Lord, and in the power of his might. Put on the whole armour of God, that ye may be able to stand against the wiles of the devil. For we wrestle not against flesh and blood, but against principalities, against powers, against the rulers of the darkness of this world, against spiritual wickedness in high places. Wherefore take unto you the whole armour of God, that ye may be able to withstand in the evil day, and having done all, to stand. Stand therefore, having your loins girt about with truth, and having on the breastplate of righteousness; and your feet shod with the preparation of the gospel of peace; above all, taking the shield of faith, wherewith ye shall be able to quench all the fiery darts of the wicked. And take the helmet of salvation, and the sword of the Spirit, which is the word of God: Praying always with all prayer and supplication in the Spirit, and watching thereunto with all perseverance and supplication for all saints; (KJV, 2025).

Artwork from Shutterstock (shutterstock_1230408019)

Artwork from Shutterstock (Shutterstock—470199143)

Definition of the Spiritual Warrior's Outfit:

1) **Gird your loins (waist) with truth**—the truth of the gospel of Christ keeps us in line. We must gird ourselves with the truth of the scripture and agree that we will never stray from those words or compromise for money, friends, popularity, or politics.

2) **Breast Plate of Righteousness** (the word of God planted in your heart and mind will protect you, keeping your motives pure and honest before God. The Breast Plate of Righteousness also protects our hearts from the temptations of Satan. If the word is planted in us, we will not desire the things Satan tempts us with. God's word will keep us centered and spiritually grounded.

3) **Gird your feet with the gospel of peace** (Jesus' message of salvation and forgiveness) that we can help spread the good news of the gospel of Jesus Christ to the world where we live and our families. If we share Jesus' teachings, we can help others live victoriously. Some people preach from a pulpit or on TV. Others write books and movie scripts. Regardless of how you share the good news, it will impact someone, and maybe the one thought or quote that helps them choose to follow Christ.

4) **Shield of Faith** (perfect love casts out all fear—fear is the only thing that can destroy faith!). We strengthen our faith by studying God's word and cultivating good thoughts in our minds, rather than

embracing corrupt and evil lifestyles that include foul language. Our faith becomes our shield because it helps us block Satan's attempts to discourage us, cause us to fear things and people, or desire things that are not good for us. The shield of faith is the first defense. Then the helmet of salvation quotes scriptures at Satan, rebuking him so that he will flee from us. Then the breastplate of righteousness protects our hearts from desiring the evil thrown at us by using God's words to help us defy Satan and put him behind us.

5) **The Helmet of Salvation (memorized scriptures) helps us protect our minds and thoughts from evil desires, keeping us focused on the things God desires for us and the work for His** kingdom. We aim to reach as many people as possible and help them on their journey to heaven. If our helmet of salvation is not full of scriptures, when Satan fires negative, evil, or sinful thoughts into our mind, they will penetrate. The helmet of salvation helps to shield us from the darts thrown by Satan.

6) **Sword of the Spirit** (the word of God) is like a two-edged sword. It cuts sometimes. It is always there to help us defend ourselves against Satan and all the principalities of darkness. Combining the word of God with prayer helps us to persevere to the end, regardless of what Satan sends our way. We end up with faith like Job!

Even though the analogy of the warrior's armor may seem simple and dated, it remains relevant to us today in many more ways. If you can imagine us in a sci-fi movie fighting alien forces from outer space (demonic spirits and principalities of darkness), then you would expect the movie writers to give us armor to fight the enemy that would be superior to their guns and artillery.

Once you envision that scene, you can integrate the soldiers' armor with the concept of spiritual warfare and incorporate it into your heart. It is essential for us to get up each morning and put on the whole armor of God (spiritually) so that we can go into the day and face the principalities of the darkness of this world and walk away victorious in Christ at the end of the day.

Our daily goal is to be equipped with the spiritual tools to deal with whatever Satan throws in our path. Only then can we walk away victorious like Job did, with double what he lost restored to him.

As you learn more about spiritual warfare, you will begin to see how easily the spirit of "Jannes and Jambre" can infiltrate our lives and churches.

Even though the spirit that opposed Moses is more than four thousand years old, it remains very active today in every aspect of the world, including politics, academia, spiritual arenas, new age groups, political analysis, and church leadership.

I pray that the thoughts I have shared with you in this book will help you prepare to be a spiritual warrior in these last days. No matter where you are in your journey spiritually, remember one thing: "Greater is he who is living inside of us than he who is in the world—and our protector (Jesus) has made a way of escape for us—always ensuring we win over evil if we trust him with our whole heart!"

The Spirit of Jannes and Jambres' effect on the Pastor

Once Satan determines that he needs to send in the spirit of Jannes and Jambres to help out other controlling spirits like the Leviathan spirit in your church, the dynamics of leadership will change. Every time I talk with a pastor about these spirits and counsel them on how they can discern and block these spirits, I hear the following questions:

1) How can I determine if the spirit of Jannes and Jambres is affecting one of my church members?
2) How can I determine if this spirit is influencing people on my leadership team?
3) How can I know if this spirit is affecting me (the pastor)?
4) How can I stop this spirit's influence and control?
5) If this spirit is not in my church, how can I ensure it does not get in my church and take control?

This is the reply I gave to these pastors. This same answer is appropriate even if you are a church member and you discern this spirit operating in your church's leadership team or pastor.

When this spirit begins working in your church and you recognize it, you must start a fast. I recommend fasting for at least three days before attempting to confront this spirit. If this spirit works through more than one person trying to gain control in your church, you must fast for at least seven days. This spirit is very powerful. It can replicate an actual move of God almost to perfection. It can deceive over 70 percent of evangelicals and over 90 percent of non-evangelicals.

To properly assess and identify the individuals under the control of this spirit, you need to analyze their actions, motives, and characteristics. Please pay close attention to the manipulations it is performing. Analyze the "powers" it has demonstrated in your church services, members, and leaders, comparing those demonstrations to the actions of the real power of God. Identify the points of deception to triangulate the actual area of concern. This spirit tends to attack from multiple angles. It helps to camouflage its proper course of action.

The spirit of Jannes and Jambres loves to counterfeit the real power of God and demonstrate it with such charisma that the majority of the church community would not recognize its plan of deception. It is crucial to assess the amount of spiritual power that this spirit is portraying. This is a key factor in determining if the human host for this spirit is oppressed or possessed by the spirit. The more there is a display of spiritual power in the service, the greater the risk of this spirit acting out if the person(s) you are dealing with are possessed.

The best example of this type of demonstration that I can share is to describe for you how this spirit affected a pastor's wife I dealt with several years ago. The pastor and his wife started this church. They wanted their two sons and daughter to be automatically grandfathered into the church's senior leadership. They wanted them to continue to control the influx of money and continue to live their exorbitant lifestyle when they and their wives were retired or dead. They structured the church like a limited liability partnership, blocking and preventing all outside influence in the management of the church.

Then, they formed a trust and other legal documents to ensure that the church membership could never gain control or have a board of directors installed. All legal documents, filings, and money were contained within the family. They did not share the finances with the church or demonstrate accountability for their actions.

As this couple reached 60, they began transitioning their children into positions. They remained completely involved in the day-to-day activity of the church to ensure that no one else influenced their children or gained any control.

However, they had not noticed a growing relationship between their daughter and another lady in the church. This lady was old enough to be their daughter's mother. She was a widow and appeared to be a devout prayer warrior. She was active in several groups at the church and always willing to help in any way she could. This pastor and his wife never noticed that this lady had a genuine relationship with God and had the gift of tongues and interpretation active in her life. She never spoke in tongues during church services. She was quiet and shy, but loving.

The closer this lady got to their daughter, the more she began interceding for the daughter. As she shared scriptures and insights with the daughter, she pointed out areas of dedication and shared "God-ideas" with the pastor's daughter. They watched as their daughter grew closer to God, and they were pleased. Then the Holy Spirit began showing their daughter things. Her faith grew, and her connection with God became stronger. One day, the Lord showed the daughter something the family was doing wrong. God showed her that it was spiritual witchcraft and that it would keep them from going in the rapture. So, the daughter shared this with her parents, not realizing that the Spirits of Jannes and Jambres had been controlling her mother, along with the spirit of Leviathan, for over twenty years.

When the daughter finished sharing with her parents and church leaders what they needed to do as a family and as a church to correct this problem, the preacher's wife went into orbit. The demons that had appeared to be dormant and only oppressing her on rare occasions was actually a full-blown demonic possession case.

The pastor's wife had played with various spirits, compromising and manipulating others to her advantage. She could secure any amount of money they needed for any reason. She knew how to work the crowd. This spirit became so angry toward this widow that she went on a full attack on her in the church and the community. She began spreading lies about this lady, trying to discredit her testimony.

The result of the pastor's wife's charade was the complete destruction of this widow in the church. People refused to sit near her or talk with her. So, the lady left the church and stayed at home, watching the church online. Local law enforcement officers were even called in and asked to arrest this lady for sexual misconduct toward their daughter (27 years old). Of course, those accusations were false, and by the time she was cleared of them, she had lost her job, home, and car. She had no option but to go to a nursing home, which is where she died four years later, of a broken heart.

When combined with other spirits, such as Leviathan, Python, Jezebel, and other legendary host spirits, this spirit can possess life-destroying, ministry-destroying, and career-destroying capabilities if you are unaware of how to bind them. Spiritual warfare is real. Satan is fighting with everything he has to get everyone possible out of the church in these last days. Satan also wants to stop our testimony. He is more afraid of what our effective prayer lives will do to destroy this kingdom than he is of most church leaders and their sermons.

I have shared many facts about this church and family with you. I hope you understand these facts about spirits, especially that they can lie dormant for years, controlling an individual, and gradually increasing control prevents the person from realizing that they have transitioned from being oppressed to being possessed. All spirits love to rock us to sleep spiritually and gain control over our lives without our recognition. If Satan came to your front door, rang the doorbell, and introduced himself when we opened the door, 100% of us would slam the door shut in his face and run. So, he has to sneak in quietly and slowly, inch by inch!

Key Characteristics that are present with all spirits:

1) Selfishness, self-centeredness, neediness
2) Greed, covetousness, and stealing
3) Lying, deceitfulness, and manipulation
4) Control, always forcing their ideas and plans on others
5) Always feels that their way is best—never willing to let others control
6) Never willing to let others try their methods
7) Must be involved in all things money in the church
8) Must be involved in all activities of the church
9) Demonstrates and behaves like they are better than everyone else
10) Their personal testimonies will have hidden in them somewhere how good they are, how righteous they have been, and they are constantly trying to convince you that they do not sin.
11) If you pay close attention, you will notice that the person who is host to these spirits always gets even with anyone they think has harmed them.
12) Retaliates always and lets everyone know that they retaliated.
13) When the spirit is operating in or on them, they are loud and boisterous
14) The hosts of these spirits are always "victims" and never do anything wrong themselves.
15) They are incapable of taking the blame and walking away for the sake of peace. They never "take one" for the team!

Summary of the seven steps I have discussed with you:

1) Discernment
2) Assess and identify all individuals involved
3) Assess the amount of "spiritual power" this spirit demonstrates.

4) Serious Fasting
5) Intercessory Prayer
6) Read your Bible and search all scriptures you need to quote when confronting this spirit or the individuals controlled by these spirits.
7) Design a spiritual warfare plan to help you combat these spirits daily and the retaliating spirits that follow them. We must learn how to fight spiritually both defensively and offensively. We cannot reach out and bind a spirit or cast a spirit out without a defensive plan to protect ourselves, our families, and our homes. Satan does not play fair!

I pray that I have been able to explain this spirit and how it operates, so that you can benefit from the knowledge God has given me about the spirit realm and how to engage in spiritual warfare. We must maintain a strong prayer life rooted in the Word of God. We must fight to survive in these last days. I am not a preacher who runs around finding demons everywhere and saying that everyone is possessed. However, I must admit that in an attempt to fit in better, all of us Pentecostal evangelicals have downplayed the spiritual warfare and demon possession teachings of our faith. Most of us completely shut down teaching on this topic. It made it easier for us to be accepted in other churches. I was guilty of this myself.

After going through the greatest trial of my life, I realized that I could have avoided the worst of it if I had been in my war room, following the seven steps I listed above. However, when God got through bringing me through that "tight place," no one, not even my family, could stop me from spiritual warfare. We can live victoriously. It is up to us. We are going to be tried and tested. Jesus told us that his chosen would be tried and tested—put through the fire. But if we keep our faith and put on the whole armor of God each day, God has promised us that he will bring us through. We may be battle-scarred, but we will be victorious!

Keep the faith! Do not let fear in! Stay in God's word daily!

I want to share with you a quote from ***"Broken: Braced for Favor"*** (Blackmon, 2022). I think this will encourage you. If you feel that you are broken or damaged, I recommend you begin this series. It is available on Amazon. Two books have been released in this series annually since 2022.

FAITH

"Faith is daring your mind and heart to believe what everyone else says is impossible. Even if your mind says you cannot do it, but your heart believes, faith will allow you to dance on the grave of doubt and be victorious.

Faith is not listening to gossip and the opinions of others, especially negative comments and advice. Faith is choosing to praise God when everyone is crying and in despair.

Faith is choosing to rejoice and dance in the presence of your enemies because you know the Holy Ghost has you covered with the blood of Jesus Christ. Faith dances in the face of death. Faith sings when you feel like crying.

Faith marches forward when every bone in your body cries to stop and sit down. Faith smiles while the tears flow down your face. Faith praises God through tears and broken hearts. Faith does not stop because things look impossible. Faith believes in God, even though you cannot hear or see Him.

Faith drowns out negative thoughts and laughs when others say you are crazy because what you believe in appears to be impossible.

Faith believes that all things are possible through Jesus Christ and chooses to dance in the middle of the trial because faith knows that the God you serve loves to show up and show out!

Remember, Jesus defeated death, hell, and the grave. So, faith allows you to join him as he dances on the devil's grave in advance, while you praise God for the victory!

La Wanda Blackmon (2022)
Broken: Braced for Favor

I hope these words about faith are helpful to you. Where faith is, doubt does not exist. Where doubt is in control, fear cannot enter! If Satan cannot get us to fear, he loses the largest part of the battle for our minds.

Study and put on the whole armor of God. Write a spiritual warfare prayer for your situation and use it daily to defeat Satan. Write the scriptures that speak life, deliverance, healing, and faith into your situation and post them in a visible place in your house. Place them where you will see them each day and be reminded that God has you in the palm of his hand and that with all you commit to him, he will protect you, including you!

Write to us and let us know if this book has helped you. We want to hear from you. Send us your prayer request, and we will post them in our "War Room," where we pray daily. There is unity and power in corporate prayer!

Your prayer partner and friend in Christ,

Tommy and La Wanda Blackmon

 ## About the Author

LaWanda Blackmon is a published author in the genres of healthcare-related and evangelical ministry. She has published over 19 medical books, more than 100 workbooks, eight religious books, ten devotional books, and prayer journals before beginning *The Redeeming Love Series*.

LaWanda was given this series by the Lord—it was born from the hurt, pain, abandonment, unfair punishment, and betrayal she suffered at the hands of those closest to her. As she laid her hurt and scars at Jesus' feet, he taught her how to love those who had falsely accused her and tried to take her down.

As she grew in her spiritual relationship, her love for others, including her enemies, deepened. She was able to forgive each of her accusers as they began to die and call her to ask for forgiveness. In this series, each book addresses the points outlined in "***Broken: Braced for Favor***" (2022). Mrs. Blackmon will take you on a journey from Broken to Redeemed as she shows you what it means to have God break you, humble you, and then redeem you as his own!

Before she finished this series, she was contacted by HFT Publishing and asked to write a book series on the book of Revelation. This series is called *"Revelation: Made Simple Series."*

The first book she wrote for this series was "***Revelation Made Simple: The Greatest Love Letter to the church from Jesus Christ.***"

The second book, "***Revelation Made Simple: Learn what God wants you to know from this mysterious book that will help you be 'Rapture-Ready!'***"

The third book, **"Revelation Made Simple: Rapture Ready Study Companion,"** was designed as a companion to the first two books in this series. The key concepts and information

The fourth book in this series, **"Revelation Made Simple: The Tribulation Period and Our Future Explained,"** is currently in the initial editing phase, with a publication date scheduled for Fall 2026.

She has begun working on the fifth book on Revelation, **"Revelation Made Simple: The In-Depth Chronological Events of Revelation."** This book will examine the book of Revelation in chronological order, supporting the information with prophecies from the Old Testament. (Anticipated publication date: Spring 2027). Each book builds on the previous one. As you progress through the series, you will be provided with increasingly detailed information to help you become a victorious spiritual warrior as we draw closer to the rapture of the church and the end of the days.

This book, **"Jannes and Jambre: Opposing Moses before Pharaoh**, is not a part of a series. It is an unusual style book for this author. La Wanda was inspired to write this short book as an encouragement tool to help individuals who want to know more about spiritual warfare, but the thought of studying it scares them. This book deals with this one spirit and how it opposed Moses and Aaron when they were trying to help the children of Israel get out of Egypt and out from under slavery.

The next book to be published by this author will be out by the end of Summer 2025: **"Are you really the Bride of Christ or are you just dating him for the blessings**?" This is a short book as well. It is designed to help you examine your Christian life, assess your current standing and direction, and identify the necessary changes to make you rapture-ready. It is hard for us to evaluate ourselves effectively. We believe that we are justified in our actions and are confident that God will understand our intentions.

Author's Credentials and Experience:

Mrs. Blackmon has over 35 years of experience in nursing and has been preaching since she was 16 years old. She became a licensed minister with the Assemblies of God in 1991. She has been ordained for over 15 years. Her heart has always been devoted to medical missions, both domestically and internationally. She loves teaching in ministry and her career as well.

However, since 2019, she has seen a shift in the focus of her ministry. The Holy Spirit has led her to write books for pastors, church leaders, and individuals who desire to be in ministry. As a result, pastors are now calling her the "prophetic voice for Pastors."

Her education includes a two-year registered nursing training program, a double major (Associate of Science), and an Associate of Arts degree. She also has two Bachelor of Science degrees (Nursing and Liberal Arts). Ms. Blackmon has two master's degrees (Nursing and Education). Her doctoral work has been in medical research and education.

Her work experience spans the full spectrum of nursing and nursing leadership, including consulting and freelance writing. Her passion for education is her greatest asset, as she strives to reach as many people as possible with the message of Jesus each year.

You can reach her at:

La Wanda Blackmon
P. O. Box 712
Brewton, AL 36427-0712
lawanda@minister.com

HFT Publishing
P.O. Box 1873
Brewton, AL 36427
HFT-Publishing@post.com

Check back with Amazon every 90 days to see if more books by this author have been added. HFT Publishing, Inc. adds books from its authors monthly in paperback and Kindle formats. Mrs. Blackmon's books are produced on a routine schedule. The publisher typically posts a new one every 90 days, as she has two series in production. Most of her books end up being college and university curricula and textbooks across America. Those books are in hardback covers for durability. The other books are not published in hardcover due to cost. She wants to keep all books as affordable as possible so that they can reach as many people worldwide as possible.

Check out her "***Redeeming Love***" Series and the "***Revelation—Made Simple***" books if you have not read those. If you wish to purchase books in bulk for use in your church's Bible study groups or Sunday school classes, please get in touch with HFT Publishing via fax at (251-248-2709) with a written request. List the name of the book and the quantity needed. They will fax you a quote.

 ## Other Books by this Author

Closer to Jesus Devotional Series: (10-Book Series)

1) (2020) ***Getting to know God through the Old Testament: Genesis to Ezra Devotional*** (90-day devotional)
2) (2020) ***Getting to know God through the Old Testament: Genesis to Ezra Prayer Journal***
3) (2021) ***Learning about God through the Eyes of the Old Testament Prophets: Nehemiah to Malachi Devotional*** (90-day devotional)
4) (2021) ***Learning about God through the Eyes of the Old Testament Prophets: Nehemiah to Malachi Prayer Journal***
5) (2022) ***Meeting Jesus through the eyes of the New Testament—Matthew to Romans Devotional*** (90-day devotional)
6) (2022) ***Meeting Jesus through the eyes of the New Testament—Matthew to Romans Prayer Journal***
7) (2023) ***Walking with Power like in the New Testament Churches—Galatians to I John Devotional*** (90-day devotional)
8) (2023) ***Walking with Power like in the New Testament Churches—Galatians to I John Prayer Journal***
9) (2024) ***Preparing to Meet Jesus in the New Testament—II John to Revelation Devotional*** (90-day devotional)
10) (2024) ***Preparing to Meet Jesus in the New Testament—II John to Revelation Prayer Journal***

Non-Series Books: (5 Books)

 ***Jannes and Jambres:*** *Opposing Moses before Pharaoh* (2024)

Are you really the Bride of Christ or just dating him for the blessings? (2024)

Can America come back COVID-19, election Fraud & Terrorism? *Learn What the Future Holds* (2025)

What is wrong with the church? *"One More Night with the Frogs" Syndrome* (2025)

Where are the warriors? *I have left this pea patch for the last time!* (2026)

    Check Amazon Monthly to see which books have been added. All books will be converted to Kindle format. Currently, we do not have conversion and publication dates available. The priority is paperback print. The books on contracts with colleges and universities for textbooks will be made available to students in Kindle and hardcover formats. Those texts will be the first ones converted to Kindle eBook format.

Revelation: Made Simple Series: (5-book series)

**Revelation Made Simple**: *The greatest love letter to the church from Jesus Christ* (2022)

**Revelation Made Simple**: *Learning What God wants you to know from this mysterious book that will help you to be rapture-ready* (2023)

**Revelation Made Simple**: *Rapture-Ready Study Companion* (2024)

Revelation Made Simple: *The tribulation and our future explained* (2025)

Revelation Made Simple: *The In-depth chronological events of Revelation* (2026)

Redeeming Love Series: (60 Book Series)

Book #	Letter	Book Title
1	B	**Broken**: *Braced for Favor* (2020)
2		**Broken**: *Braced for Favor Journal*

Book #	Letter	Book Title
3		**Broken:** *Braced for Favor Devotional*
4	*R*	**Redeemed:** *Forgiven and Forgotten (2021)*
5		**Redeemed:** *Forgiven and Forgotten Journal*
6		**Redeemed:** *Forgiven and Forgotten Devotional*
7	*O*	**Opened-Up:** *Stirred Up for Change (2022)*
8		**Opened-Up:** *Stirred Up for Change Journal*
9		**Opened-Up:** *Stirred Up for Change Devotional*
10	*K*	**Knocked Down:** *But not out (2023)*
11		**Knocked Down:** *But not out Journal*
12		**Knocked Down:** *But not out Devotional*
13	*E*	**Enriched:** *Exchange Your Evil Heart for a Good Heart (2024)*
14		**Enriched:** *Exchange Your Evil Heart for a Good Heart Journal*
15		**Enriched:** *Exchange Your Evil Heart for a Good Heart Devotional*
16	*N*	**New Creation:** *Now we are New Through Jesus (2025)*
17		**New Creation:** *Now we are New Through Jesus Journal*
18		**New Creation:** *Now we are New Through Jesus Devotional*
19	*B*	**Begotten:** *We belong to Jesus now (2026)*
20		**Begotten:** *We belong to Jesus now Journal*
21		**Begotten:** *We belong to Jesus now Devotional*
22	*R*	**Resurrected:** *Our Old Man is New in Christ (2026)*
23		**Resurrected:** *Our Old Man is New in Christ Journal*
24		**Resurrected:** *Our Old Man is New in Christ Devotional*
25	*A*	**Appointed:** *For a Time Like This (2026)*
26		**Appointed:** *For a Time Like This Journal*

Jannes & Jambre: Opposing Moses before Pharoah

Book #	Letter	Book Title
27		**Appointed**: *For a Time Like This Devotional*
28	*C*	**Chosen**: *Anointed for this Job (2027)*
29		**Chosen**: *Anointed for this Job Journal*
30		**Chosen**: *Anointed for this Job Devotional*
31	*E*	**Exodus**: *From our Moab to the land of plenty (2027)*
32		**Exodus**: *From our Moab to the land of plenty Journal*
33		**Exodus**: *From our Moab to the land of plenty Devotional*
34	*D*	**Deliverance**: *The Broken Delivered and Set Free (2027)*
35		**Deliverance**: *The Broken Delivered and Set Free Journal*
36		**Deliverance**: *The Broken Delivered and Set Free Devotional*
37	*F*	**Forgiven**: *Mercy and Grace (2028)*
38		**Forgiven**: *Mercy and Grace Journal*
39		**Forgiven**: *Mercy and Grace Devotional*
40	*O*	**Obedience:** *The Obedient Overcome (2028)*
41		**Obedience:** *The Obedient Overcome Journal*
42		**Obedience:** *The Obedient Overcome Devotional*
43	*R*	**Rejuvenation:** *Restored and Rejuvenated Church (2028)*
44		**Rejuvenation:** *Restored and Rejuvenated Church Journal*
45		**Rejuvenation:** *Restored and Rejuvenated Church Devotional*
46	*F*	**Favored**: *Unmerited Faith and Favor (2029)*
47		**Favored**: *Unmerited Faith and Favor Journal*
48		**Favored**: *Unmerited Faith and Favor Devotional*

Book #	Letter	Book Title
49	A	**Anointed:** *Adopted and Betrothed (2029)*
50		**Anointed:** *Adopted and Betrothed Journal*
52	V	**Victorious:** *Living Victoriously in God's Favor (2029)*
53		**Victorious:** *Living Victoriously in God's Favor Journal*
54		**Victorious:** *Living Victoriously in God's Favor Devotional*
55	O	**Opportunities:** *Your Divine Purpose (2030)*
56		**Opportunities:** *Your Divine Purpose Journal*
57		**Opportunities:** *Your Divine Purpose Devotional*
58	R	**Restoration:** *Restored and Rapture Ready (2030)*
59		**Restoration:** *Restored and Rapture Ready Journal*
60		**Restoration:** *Restored and Rapture Ready Devotional*

This author has written a total of 80 religious books. The book titles, concepts, ideas, outlines, and related materials have been copyrighted and are awaiting a print date. Some books were written years ago but never published. They are currently being updated with current events and will be published during the year listed in parentheses.

All of these books, including reprints previously published by other companies, as well as future books, have been copyrighted to La Wanda Blackmon and her estate. HFT Publishing, Inc. has signed a contract for 100 books that will be printed and sold on Amazon as part of a joint venture project. This will put the dynamic works of this author into the hands of more people than she would ever be able to reach through a pulpit alone.

References

Anchor Bible Dictionary. (1992). *The Anchor Bible Dictionary*, ed. David Noel Freedman. New York, NY: Doubleday.

BibleGateway, 2024. *Encyclopedia of the Bible* [word and topic searches]. Retrieved on 2-20-2024 from website: *www.biblegateway.com/resources/encyclopedia-of-the-bible/* (topic of search).

Blackmon, L. (2020). *Getting to know God through the Old Testament: Genesis to Ezra*. Brewton, AL: HFT Publishing

Blackmon, L. (2022). *Broken: Braced for Favor*. Brewton, AL: HFT Publishing

Blackmon, L. (2023). *Revelation Made Simple: The greatest love letter to the church from Jesus Christ*. Brewton, AL: HFT Publishing

Blair, L. (2024). *Over half of American pastors have considered quitting*. Retrieved on 5-23-2024 from ChristianPost.com at https://www.christianpost.com/news/over-half-American-pastors-have-considered-quitting-poll.html

Downey, R. & Burnett, M. (2013). *A story of God and all of us: A novel based on the epic TV miniseries 'The Bible.'* New York, NY: Faith Words- Hachette Book Group

Hagee, M. (2023). *Spiritual Warfare: Unlock the Supernatural and Access the Promises of God*. Southlake, TX: Breakfast for Seven

HoustonHerald.com (2024). [Original: 2019, Jan 2/Updated 2024, Feb 20]. *Thousands of churches are closing every year in the US*. Retrieved on May 20, 2024, from: *https://houstonherald.com/2023/01/thousands-of-churches-closing-every-year-in-u-s/*

Hybel, B. (2008). *Too busy not to pray: Special Edition-20th Anniversary*. Downer Grove, IL: Intervarsity Press.

Jacobs, L. (2012, October 11). *Last days revival or end time apostasy?* Retrieved from https://www.shema.com/last-days-revival-or-end-time-apostassssy-208/

Jing, Z. (2019, June 23). *The last days are here: Are you prepared to meet God? Retrieved from* https://www.holyspiritsspeaks.org/testimonies/prepare-to-meet-God/

Johnson, J. (2019). *The power of consecration: A prophetic word to the church.* Shippensburg, PA: Destiny Image.

Johnson, J. (2023). *The Warrior Bride.* Shippensburg, PA: Destiny Image

LeClaire, J. (2020). *Discerning Prophetic Witchcraft: Exposing the supernatural divination that is deceiving spiritually hungry believers.* Shippensburg, PA: Destiny Image

LeClaire, J. (2021a). *Cleansing your home from evil:* Kick the Devil out of your House. Shippensburg, PA: Destiny Image

LeClaire, J. (2021b). *The making of a watchman: Practical Training for Prophetic Prayer and Powerful Intercession.* Shippensburg, PA: Destiny Image

OakRidgeBibleChapel.org. (2021). Jezebel or Jesus? The church at Thyatira [July 21, 2021 Online Sermon by Lew Worrad]. Retrieved from https://oakridgebiblechapel.org/jezebel-or-jesus/(Retrieved on 4-20-2023).

O'Neal, C. (2019). *A word from God for the church.* Brewton, AL: HFT Publishing

O'Neal, C. (2020). *"Why am I not living a victorious life?"* Brewton, AL: HFT Publishing

O'Neal, C. (2021). *"The Spiritual Warrior."* Brewton, AL: HFT Publishing

Shutterstock (2025). Artwork inside the manuscript. Paid for and licensed from Shutterstock to La Wanda Blackmon. Retrieved from https://www.shutterstock.com

Stone, P. (2011). *Purging your house, pruning your family tree: How to rid your home and family of demonic influence and generational oppressions.* Lake Mary, FL: Charisma House.

Stone, P. (2013). *The Judas goat.* Lake Mary, FL: Charisma House.

Swaggart, J. (2011). *I've left this pea patch for the last time.* [Sermon-posted 20 Mar 2011]. YouTube video. Retrieved from: https://www.bing.com/videos/riverview/relatedvideo?q=where+is+the+scripture+in+the+bible+that+says+I+have+left+my+pea+patch+my+last+time&mid=6BE6EB2ED4B195E407AC6BE6EB2ED4B195E407AC&FORM=VIRE

Woods, M. (2024). *The Truth* [song lyrics]. Brentwood, TN: Fair Trade Service Record Label

www.ingramcontent.com/pod-product-compliance
Lightning Source LLC
Chambersburg PA
CBHW050648160426
43194CB00010B/1861